POLITICAL
WIVES

POLITICAL WIVES

THE LIVES OF THE SAINTS

Susan Riley

DENEAU

DENEAU & WAYNE PUBLISHERS LTD.
760 BATHURST STREET
TORONTO, ONTARIO
M5S 2R6

© 1987
Printed in Canada

This book has been published with the assistance of the Canada Council and
Ontario Arts Council under their block grant programs.

CANADIAN CATALOGUING IN PUBLICATION DATA

Riley, Susan, 1947-
Political wives

ISBN 0-88879-170-4 (bound)
ISBN 0-88879-172-0 (pbk.)

1. Politicians' wives – Canada.   2. Wives – Effect of
husband's employment on.   I. Title.

FC601.A1R54 1987   971.064'092'2   C87-094579-3
F1034.3.A2R54 1987

For my mother

CONTENTS

ACKNOWLEDGMENTS   ix

PREFACE   xi

ONE: *The importance of being earnest*   1

TWO: *Breaking every rule*   21

THREE: *An unhappy interlude*   45

FOUR: *Shopping your way to the top*   71

FIVE: *The miracle of hairspray*   93

SIX: *Amazing grace*   115

SEVEN: *A commendable failure*   135

EIGHT: *Living with conflict*   151

NINE: *Alternate wifestyles*   161

CONCLUSION: *Transcending wifedom*   181

ACKNOWLEDGMENTS

I AM VERY GRATEFUL TO Joyce Wayne for suggesting this book to me and for helping me complete it. I especially appreciate the tact, delicacy and unflagging enthusiasm she brought to the project.

I also want to thank senior management at the *Ottawa Citizen*, where I work, for giving me time off to complete this book. In particular, I am grateful to Keith Spicer, Nelson Skuce and Graham Parley for their interest in the project and for their encouragement.

I would also like to thank friends and colleagues who gave me suggestions, ideas and encouragement, especially Wendy Warburton, Judy Morrison, Jane O'Hara, Eileen Donoghue, Sherri Barron, Prudence Craib and Mary Trueman. I also appreciate the candor of the various political wives I talked to in confidential interviews, and the insights offered by politicians, male and female.

Above all, I would like to thank Mary Hutton for her faith, her forbearance, her editorial judgment and for some of the funniest lines in the book. She bolstered my confidence and my spirits all the way to the last page.

PREFACE

AT FIRST, I WANTED TO CALL this book *The Miracle of Hair Spray: A Survival Guide for Political Wives.* A friend suggested calling it *Little Women,* and I liked that, too, although it had a slightly familiar ring.The same friend suggested *Talk Softly and Marry a Big Prick,* but I didn't want any trouble with customs. I briefly considered *Fatuousness as a Feminist Issue* and *The Man Who Mistook his Wife for a Vote,* but those titles were also too derivative. So I finally settled on a compromise: *Political Wives: The Lives of the Saints.*

The indecision I suffered over the title plagued me throughout the entire book. I was never sure what tone to strike. On one hand, my own nature and a lifetime in political journalism have enabled me to be both glib and superficial across a whole range of topics. There is no subject that I cannot trivialize. And what lends itself to trivialization more naturally than political wives?

To me, there has always been something innately hilarious about the political wife in full professional flight. Funny in the way that tri-coloured sandwiches cut in

triangles are funny. Funny in the way that fully robed
Supreme Court judges caught in a windstorm are funny.
Political wives are like afternoon tea dances, or the Queen
Mother; familiar yet foreign. I feel for them the same
nostalgic contempt I feel for beauty pageants and formal
weddings. I close my eyes and think political wife, and
I see P.G. Wodehouse.

On the other hand, when I sat down to write I ran
into problems right away. For one thing, I didn't want
to be mean. I wanted to be fair, and fairness is the death
of humour. I know some of the women I am writing
about. I don't mean that we are friends or that we have
even had any significant conversations. But, as a journalist, I have watched Mila, Maureen, Geills and Margaret — and countless other wives from the lower ranks
— at close hand. I have reported their public utterances,
competed for world exclusives on their banquet menus
(this was during my newsmagazine days) and puzzled
over their macro-political effect. I have heard all the
gossip — sympathetic, unkind, sexist and some of it
true. And I have a sense that these women aren't caricatures but people, complex, often intelligent people,
no more evil or ridiculous than anyone else.

The minute I start thinking like this the humour bleeds
out of me, quips and one-liners withering as I contem-
plate my moral obligation to living souls. I tell myself
that if I'm not careful I'll end up writing one of those
breathey, awestruck paeons that *Chatelaine* magazine once
specialized in. (This trend reached its peak in 1986, when

Chatelaine declared Mila Mulroney Woman of the Year.)
I didn't want to be that kind.

What always brought me smartly to my senses during
these arguments with myself was the realization that
however human, however quaint, however hilarious they
might be, political wives — at least the active ones —
are an embarrassment and disgrace to us all. They allow
themselves be used by our political culture to express
certain noxious ideas about the role of women, about
marriage and about family. However subtle, however
unwilling, however low-profile they might be, they
embody a patriarchal notion of female virtue which
involves trading off personal power for reflected glory.
"They're hookers," one friend said dismissively. "Upper-class hookers." I told her that was harsh. Real prosti-
tutes work much harder for their money than political
wives do, under much inferior conditions.

Nonetheless her remark called to mind a possibly
apocryphal story about Evita Peron who was heckled
on an official visit to northern Italy. "Did you hear them
call me a whore?" Evita demanded indignantly of her
naval escort. "Think nothing of it, Señora," the escort
replied gallantly. "I haven't been to sea for fifteen years
and they still call me an admiral."

To get back to this book. This isn't a book of reportage.
I had no interest in gathering up the carefully laundered
anecdotes and evasive generalities of a dozen political
wives into a volume of unsurpassed banality. (Although
that, too, is well within my capabilities.) In my experience, interviewing political wives while they are on the

job is like playing badminton: one harmless exchange of birdies after another. The really interesting answers to the really interesting questions will go with most wives to their graves. Or to their publishers.

Instead, *Lives of the Saints* is an attempt to analyze the phenomenon of political wife, to look at the role she plays in our political life, to examine certain well-known wives — Mila, Maureen, Margaret, Nancy — in search of some common thread, some revelation. Some of the wives I write about amuse me, some annoy me and a few enrage me. I tried to approach all of them with the same neutral curiosity with which I would approach any endangered species.

ONE

The importance of being earnest

A GUIDE TO PROPER DRESS, APPROPRIATE BEHAVIOR AND ACCEPTABLE ATTITUDES FOR PUTATIVE POLITICAL WIVES

"In matters of grave importance, style, not sincerity, is the vital thing."

OSCAR WILDE

WHAT A PITY ROGER TORY PETERSON never published a field guide to political wives. We could use an accessible little book describing their nesting habits, their natural habitat, their distinctive markings. They are such a fascinating species, as ubiquitous as seagulls or sparrows or American tourists, yet little understood and rarely studied.

Occasionally, a particularly brightly coloured wife — a Margaret Trudeau or a Jackie Kennedy — will catch the public eye. But most of the time political wives live in the background of public life, moving freely among us, but as invisible as water.

On the other hand, the *institution* of political wife is neither unimportant nor invisible. In fact, it is hard to imagine our present political culture surviving without it. Wives are as necessary to contemporary political leaders as the slaves were to the Egyptian pyramid builders. They fill some highly specialized and often undervalued functions in political life: they take on the burden of caring for others, they remind us all what it means to be a lady, they add colour to the drab gray of public life.

Some succeed more brilliantly than others, of course. Some fail. Often, there is fervent disagreement over which wife belongs on which list. For some reason Nancy Reagan, Olive Diefenbaker, Eleanor Roosevelt — as diverse a group as you're likely to find — are considered successes. Why? Why did Margaret Trudeau, Maryon Pearson and Maureen McTeer fail? Did they fail? Who decides?

By conventional standards, Mila Mulroney is a model political wife. So why is it that most of my friends, and even strangers I talk to on airplanes, can't stand her? Maureen McTeer provokes equally strong and equally contradictory emotions. So did Margaret Trudeau. Political wives are a litmus test for our attitudes about women, our attitudes as individuals and as a society.

That alone makes them interesting. So does the rich variety of behavior they exhibit. We have to wonder what *People* magazine would do without Joan Kennedy, Margaret Trudeau or Imelda Marcos. The saints get a fair amount of attention, too, of course, but, as Billy Joel says, the sinners are much more fun. They are also more useful to us, scientifically speaking. We can sense the outside limits of acceptable wifely behavior from public reaction to their blunders. Old newspaper clippings provide a sort of Richter scale of scandal, and are an invaluable resource for anyone who wants to study this species in depth.

The first question we have to ask is this: why, in 1987, are there still political wives? (This is different, of course, from asking why women marry politicians. We are speaking about wives in the upper case.) Why do we need political wives? Why do we put up with them? Why does society insist on an archetypal wife, an Every-wife, a figurehead with no political power but potent symbolic importance? What is the political wife saying about women, about marriage, about the way power is distributed in our society? It sounds as if she is saying that women are status symbols, possessions, mirrors for the men they live with. But aren't those days gone?

Are political wives really an endangered species, as I suggested rather glibly in my preface? They should be, but I'm afraid they're not. They have powerful defenders of course: their husbands, their husbands' political aides, the political *animateurs* who deal in images and impressions. For the cold-eyed operatives, wives are as inanimate and as crucial as the right campaign logo — another piece of visual imagery.

As for wives, they are remarkably adaptable creatures. They have evolved, over time, from an Olive Diefenbaker to a Margaret Trudeau to a Mila Mulroney, from an Eleanor Roosevelt to a Rosalyn Carter to a Nancy Reagan. They have changed to meet new demands. In Olive's day they had to be matronly, efficient and warm. Now they have to be sexy, efficient and warm. When confronted by a natural enemy, like feminism, they invent post-feminism. When threatened with public disapproval because of their excessive zeal in nest-feathering, for example, they make themselves socially useful. When criticized for being too politically involved, too independent-minded, too interventionist, they either move their activities indoors or have nervous breakdowns. They survive.

To discover why they survive we have to look beyond the peculiar habits of individual wives — fascinating though these may be — at the larger picture. We have to ask why the condition of being a political wife transcends petty differences of ideology, culture and nationality. We have to ask who makes the rules and why women continue to obey them.

But first, let's take a look at what we know about political wives, Let us, like serious ornithologists, consult our guidebooks. Once we understand what political wives hold in common, we can turn our attention to individual variations.

THE DRESS CODE

The key thing to remember about a political wife's wardrobe is this: *it has nothing to do with her*. It is meant to enhance or convey a political image of her husband. Jackie Kennedy may have been the most successful political wife ever because of her profound understanding of this central truth. In fact Jack once described himself as "the man who accompanied Jackie to Poland."

The overall goal is clothing that makes no statement whatsoever — fashion or political — yet avoids looking like a theatre usher's uniform. Under no circumstances should a political wife appear in public wearing a T-shirt with writing on it (Margaret Trudeau). Or anything in black leather (Joan Kennedy). Nor should she carry an umbrella emblazoned with cute slogans, or wear lace-up wrestling boots, no matter how urgently the style section of the *Village Voice* may promote them. When you look at a political wife, her clothes should say nothing more arresting than "no comment."

This middle-of-the-road style, or non-style, transcends party lines. When it comes to clothes, Lucille

Broadbent operates within the same limitations (although not necessarily within the same budget) as Geills Turner and Mila Mulroney, and Raisa Gorbachev plays by the same rules as Nancy Reagan. In the United States that means Republican cloth coats and plain lines; in Canada, it means Creeds.

When fashions are in transition (as they always are except for the Royal Family and the poor) a political wife stays just behind the newest wave. After a trend like padded shoulders, for example, is so well established that it is no longer being worn in New York, the political wife may wear it. But never before. The prudent wife opts for invisibility over novelty. As in architecture, there is an "international style" for political wives and, as in architecture, it is unimaginative, repetitive and deliberately unremarkable.

On the all-important and vexing question of hemlines, an intelligent wife will do what everyone else does and, when in doubt, wear the length she would have worn three years ago. As recently as 1977, Margaret Trudeau was criticized for appearing at an official White House function in a knee-length dress, when all the other women wore long gowns. Margaret was "doing her own thing" instead of doing the same thing as everyone else. Her mistake, one of many, was imagining that a political wife, like a normal woman, can use clothing to express something about herself. Not so. A political wife's clothes are meant, like a uniform, to disguise differences not to celebrate them.

"The big problem is to find suitable hats. I don't care for them all that much, but you have to wear them in politics," Maryon Pearson once said. Pat Nixon, a scrupulous conformist, described her philosophy of wardrobe this way: "I never choose something just because I like it. I think: Will it pack? Is it conservative enough? Can I wear it a long time?" That explains why Pat Nixon looked the way she did. Permanently pressed. It also explains why Martha Mitchell once remarked, acidly: "You'd have to build a woman like Pat Nixon." On the other hand, who was Martha Mitchell to talk?

Frowsy, frilly and flouncy, the wife of Richard Nixon's attorney-general was a fashion mistake from the top of her worm-curl hairdo to the tips of her stiletto heels. For one thing, the Southern-belle look has no place in modern political decor. Ambitious male politicians do not like their wives dressing to excess any more than they do their mistresses. The blowsiness of Martha Mitchell or the rock-hooker look of Michelle Duvalier may be okay on the cover of a best-selling biography, but not at a state dinner. As one Haitian noble sniffed about Baby Doc's trashy, young wife: "She has too many things, and she wears them all at once."

There is a crucial balance here, however. Olive Diefenbaker had only eight evening gowns to her name, but television wasn't as intrusive in the fifties as it is now and frugality was a sign of virtue rather than lack of imagination. Nowadays, eight dresses would never do. A wife who appears in public wearing the same outfit twice risks sneering references in newspaper columns, unflattering comparative photographs and, the ultimate sacrilege, damage to her husband's reputation — largely because she lives in a long-departed world in which men are judged by how well they dress their women.

On the other hand, the political wife wins no friends for herself or her husband wearing budget fabrics. No one knows this better than Geills Turner, who must get family rates at Ralph Lauren. During the 1986 convention that affirmed John Turner's leadership of the Liberal party, Turner loyalists — including Geills — wore cheap red-and-white Turner scarves draped around their necks to all the weekend's events. Several commentators remarked, approvingly, that it was the closest Geills Turner had ever been to polyester.

Imelda Marcos had a simple but ultimately self-defeating approach to wardrobe: if the shoe fits, buy it. When they liberated the Marcos' Malacanang Palace in Manila in Februray 1986, Aquino's forces found 2,700 pairs of shoes. They also discovered five hundred black push-up bras, suitcases filled with girdles, 1,500 handbags, thirty-five racks of fur coats, 1,200 designer dresses and bags of jewellry. This was a woman who bought emeralds in bulk. (Imelda's consumption wasn't only conspicuous, it was compulsive. How else to describe someone who picked up 2,000 dollars worth of gum on a casual stroll through the San Francisco Airport?) She was last seen in Hawaii shopping for army boots, but it is too soon to say if this represents a change in tactics or only in taste.

Excess was Imelda's undoing; it was especially unseemly given that the average annual wage in the Philippines is around 900 dollars. Michelle Duvalier, who married the porcine dictator of Haiti, Jean-Claude (Baby Doc) Duvalier, and immediately put him on a diet, was a credit-card abuser, too. She followed the trail blazed by Imelda and Evita Peron before her, spending millions on clothes and other baubles in London, Paris and New York. Michelle even invested 75,000 dollars in a freezer for her fur coats. Isn't it lucky that Haiti's climate doesn't often require fur coats? Otherwise, life would be miserable indeed for all those coatless Haitians struggling to get by on eighty dollars a year.

The sheer scale of Michelle and Imelda's bad taste eventually helped drive them, and their husbands, from office. In the West, the rather prim American media labelled them "dragon ladies," and seemed to be more appalled by their runaway consumerism than by their husbands' military brutality. You don't have to look very hard to see the sexist and racist implications in that: cold, cruel women manipulating their weak husbands, bilking the national treasury and exhibiting scandalously poor taste, besides. There is a three-word reply to the specious suggestion that somehow Third World wives have cornered the market on tackiness: Tammy Faye Bakker.

Then there are the Western wives with similar impulses but smaller budgets, for whom Imelda and Michelle provide a cautionary tale. Nancy Reagan was roundly reviled in the first year of her reign for her constant parade of 5,000-dollar dresses and the 200,000 dollars worth of new china for the White House. ("The White House really badly, badly needs china.") Mila Mulroney's expensive home decorating ideas attracted national attention, too. Apparently 24 Sussex badly, badly needed 100-dollar-a-roll wallpaper. With characteristic political acuity, Brian isn't making jokes about Mila's shopping problem these days — at least not when there are reporters around.

No amount of money can buy youthful good health, which is unfortunate, since a political wife should look younger that her years and certainly younger than her husband. In Canada, this hasn't been a problem since our prime ministers seem to have a predilection for child brides. But most political wives are in their mid-forties to mid-fifties. For them, public life becomes one long exercise in damage control. Wrinkles and white hair must be avoided for as long as plausible. Poor Joan Kennedy was so anxious to stay young she resorted to cosmetic surgery, a secret she guarded more zealously than her drinking.

Olive Diefenbaker, the ideal chatelaine for the fifties, would be considered too starched, too prim, too I.O.D.E. to meet today's standards. Fashions change. The modern wife, thanks to Jackie Kennedy, has to look like an interesting sexual partner, besides being good company at a state funeral. This obsession with youth is so much a part of popular North American culture that American Vice-President George Bush's wife, Barbara, is considered a revolutionary simply because she won't dye her hair. Bush, a mild-mannered preppie by most accounts, lost his temper when an aide suggested "something had to be done" about Barbara's appearance. She remains defiantly white haired.

Geills Turner is a perfect illustration of the corollary which says that if you can't be young, be thin. Since the Jackie Kennedy epoch, stout is out for political wives — even in Russia. Nancy Reagan is so desiccated she looks pounds away from being dangerously ill. Pat Nixon was scrawny, too. These women may scream "eating disorder" at you and me, but they are only conforming to the job description devised by their husbands' aids.

APPROPRIATE INTERESTS

Once they are all dressed up, political wives need somewhere to go. They are fortunate if they have young children to give their lives focus, purpose and to provide company. Otherwise, they face long hours of grinding leisure. This may not strike everyone as a hardship, but many a political wife has turned to drink or drugs under the strain of enforced inactivity. Fortunately, there is a narrow range of outside activities so innocuous, so apolitical and so unnecessary that they are perfectly suited to the modern political wife.

Interior decorating remains the most consistently popular and widely approved pastime among political wives of all cultures. The political world sees it as an extension of the nesting instinct, which it imagines to be a quintessentially feminine phenomenon. But it isn't so much the nesting instinct as nervous energy and anxious self-justification which fuels most redecorating efforts. It gives wives something to do while their husbands are enjoying a honeymoon with someone else — the electorate. Nancy Reagan slipped from 114 to 104 pounds in those frantic first months when she was redoing the White House (thereby satisfying two requirements of her job at once). Well, it *is* a lot of floor space.

In Canada, the dining room at 24 Sussex has been repapered so many times it has probably shrunk in size. Every incumbent wife proclaims the taste of the former occupant "ghastly" and forges on with her own improvements. Maryon Pearson papered the room in ivory to cover up "that ghastly blue" that Olive had no doubt chosen to cover the "ghastly red" the previous tenants chose. The rivalry isn't always friendly. Margaret Trudeau accused Maureen McTeer of "rape and pillage" of 24 Sussex and complained of garbage in the hallways. However Maureen got the last word; she wrote *Residences*, a thorough book on Canada's official residences, which represents the thinking wife's approach to interior decorating.

A sub-branch of interior decorating is period restoration. In his recent book called *Reagan's America, Innocents At Home,* United States historian Garry Wills credits Jackie Kennedy for pioneering in this area. Wills writes:

> What would be more wifely than furnishing the nest?
> Yet [Jackie] added elements of style (and turned duty to

public largesse) by making historical display of her antiques, uniting scholarly research and popular celebra-
tion (on her own television show). It is just one example
of many victories for the Kennedy style of public relations that, after Mrs. Kennedy, a wife could no more
afford to be without her project than a President could
afford to be without a wife.

In a typically modest Canadian adaptation, Maryon
Pearson filled a basement room at 24 Sussex with Canadiana furniture then invited journalists to photograph
her efforts. Her gesture wasn't as grand as Jackie's, but
it may have been more sincere; Maryon, after all, earned
a degree in history before she married into politics. Her
legacy to the nation was the ultimate, postwar rec room.

Shopping is still a key leisure-time activity, although
the post-Imelda wife must beware of overdoing it. In
the days when the media wasn't as intrusive as it is
now, international summits provided perfect shopping
opportunities for bored wives. While their husbands
debated exchange rates in some Venetian palace or Tok-
yo highrise, wives gleefully created their own balance-
of-payment problems in the nearby shops.

Mila never misses an opportunity to travel — particularly if Rome, Paris or New York is on the itinerary —
and, according to most accounts, she always brings her
chequebook. Nowadays, however, wives are expected
to visit hospitals or drug rehabilitation programs while
their husbands talk, primarily to give bored photographers something to shoot. This cuts severely into shopping time, and has spawned a whole generation of wives

who are secret shoppers, slinking out between good deeds and photo ops to snag another couple pair of those fabulous snakeskin shoes.

Photography (Margaret Trudeau and Geills Turner), Japanese cooking, studying French and painting are also acceptable hobbies for political wives. The important thing is that the activity not discomfit or inconvenience her husband. That rules out writing, unless the writing is drained of opinion (see Maureen McTeer's *Chatelaine* articles); social work, unless it is entirely meaningless; business, unless it is not remotely connected to politics (ditto for law); and any regular job which will not grant long frequent leaves of absence. It is really no life for an adult.

THE PROJECT

Busy-work keeps a wife out of trouble, but it will not win her acclaim. For that, she needs a project. She must conspicuously and publicly commit herself to eradicating human suffering, ending drug abuse or raising money for sick children. In North America, the project is a relatively new requirement (Wills dates it from 1961), one intended to showcase a wife's compassion and thereby reflect well on her husband. It is also meant to answer feminist criticism that wives shouldn't be mere adjuncts to their husbands. It gives her an identity separate from but not hostile to her husband's, with her own store of personal slogans and clichés. Nancy Reagan is the exemplar in this regard; her war on drug abuse a textbook example of the perfect project.

The rules for projects have shifted subtly over the years. It was once enough to care passionately about non-human victims — Lady Bird Johnson took wildflowers under her wing (so to speak) and even set aside one million dollars in her will for the National Wildflower Foundation in Texas. Today such a project wouldn't be considered sufficiently serious minded. Neither would heritage furniture. A modern wife must not be afraid to tackle our most intractable social problems — as long as she makes no attempt to actually change anything.

Her object, after all, isn't to stamp out urban poverty or drug abuse or whatever, but to generate favourable publicity — for herself and, by extension, for her husband. Nor should it be forgotten that the project illustrates not only her virtue, but her privilege. As Wills writes:

> Not until the 1960s did the upper-class institution of "the lady's charity" reach America's self-consciously middle-class ruling house. We are talking about one of the distinguishing marks of Veblen's leisure class — the langorous bestirment that marginally consumes but principally advertises a woman's conspicuous leisure.

Michelle Duvalier, Imelda Marcos and Evita Peron brought to the project the same florid style that marked their wardrobes. Michelle set up the Michelle B. Duvalier Foundation to run clinics and hospitals, but she also appeared regularly on Haitian television, dressed to the nines, handing envelopes of money to the indigent. Evita Peron did the same thing in Argentina in the forties, personally dispensing largesse to her *descamisados*. These women apparently saw no contradiction in their own immense wealth and the poverty of the people they were throwing favours to. Imelda claimed to love the poor and she was sure they loved her: "I am the little peoples' star and slave. When I go into the barrios, I get dressed up because I know the little people want to see a star."

Aside from being immensely gratifying, this kind of hands-on charity from political wives is politically useful to their husbands, and much less expensive than real social justice.

Some of the more daring wives in Ottawa have taken up the cause of Soviet Jewry or made overtures to Amnesty International, both causes that come dangerously close to being "political." However, there is an ineffectual mildness to both these efforts that make them safe — and perfect for high-minded political wives. Amnesty International deplores civil rights abuses by both left-wing and right-wing regimes, for example, and deftly avoids taking sides.

On the other hand, Tory political wife Donna Wenman, president of the Parliamentary Spouses Association, found out you can get into trouble for being too even handed. There was a minor uproar in the Commons in May 1987, when she circulated booklets referring to South Africa as "a model multiracial society."

She said she had mailed anti-apartheid material earlier and just wanted balance. As she told the press: "Unfortunately, maybe it was the wrong time to send it when the issue is as hot as it is."

Diseases are among the safest of projects, at least those which cannot be blamed on environmental or other factors. AIDS is risky, although Diana, Princess of Wales, has broken ground by being photographed in Britain holding the hand of a young man dying of the disease. Heart disease and alcoholism are also fraught with risk; a political wife who adopts these diseases risks confrontation with the powerful drug and liquor lobbies. Mila Mulroney has found a suitable charity: cystic fibrosis, an awful disease whose child victims are both blameless and photogenic.

It is still the Americans, and particularly Nancy Reagan, who lead the world in the area of conspicuous do-gooding. In 1973, on a trip to Korea, Nancy helped airlift two Korean children back to the United States for heart surgery. It was portrayed as the spontaneous gesture of a warm-hearted woman, but the lift had been carefully orchestrated. Nancy's former press secretary, Sheila Tate, told a reporter: "We had our advance people over there, looking for just that kind of situation." During a subsequent charity gala in Los Angeles, the two children appeared at Nancy's side.

Pat Nixon took on "volunteerism," a shrewd choice as Wills points out, "since the work, by its very nature, requires desultory attendance." It also fit conveniently with conservative ideology, which would like to turn over all those expensive, state-funded social services to doctors' wives with time on their hands.

ATTITUDE

A political wife can't have opinions, but she must possess attitude. What this requires is a vague, passive pleasantness alternating with a jaunty, sunny optimism. There is a generic First Lady speech in which man's inhumanity to man is deplored, the essential goodness of humankind affirmed and our great fortune to be living in such free and prosperous nation called to mind. Generally speaking, a clever political wife embraces the general and shuns the specific. For instance, she may be in favour of peace, but she may not be opposed to war.

The key attitude is public deference to her husband, private loyalty and modest refusal to take any credit for his brilliant success. "I want nothing but to be the heart of Peron," Evita once told a multitude from a balcony (naturally) in Buenos Aires.

> Because though I do my best to understand him and learn his marvellous ways, whenever he makes a decision I barely mumble. Whenever he speaks I hardly utter a single word. Whenever he gives advice I scarcely make a suggestion. What he sees, I hardly glimpse. . . .

This is a bit too abject for the contemporary wife (and it clearly raises doubts about Evita's sincerity), but you get the idea. Mila certainly does. In subtler ways she credits "Brian's government" with the single-handed salvation of the Canadian economy. Even the strong-minded Geills Turner says she would "never question" her husband in public.

For the intelligent wife, this requires a daily display of diplomacy that borders on outright fraud. Let's not be coy: a lot of these women are smarter than their husbands. The wife's dilemma is particularly acute today as feminism makes its impertinent demands. She has to be innocuous without being inane, which, as all modern examples prove, is impossible.

Now that we know the rules, it may be fitting to turn to someone who broke almost every one of them: Margaret Trudeau. In some ways Margaret was the most spectacularly inept political wife Canada has ever seen. The irony is that she was really deeply conventional—even during her periods of crazy excess.

TWO

*B*reaking every rule

HOW MARGARET TRUDEAU

BECAME THE TINA TURNER

OF POLITICAL WIFEDOM

"I'm not a weirdo, a wacko or an eccentric for wanting to do good, honest work on a day-to-day basis. I just want to find my individuality. I've had enough of being public property."

MARGARET TRUDEAU, 1978

CANADA IS A WELL-BEHAVED, even fastidious country, a country that likes to be in its fluffy pajamas by 10 p.m. most nights, watching "The National." There is even a significant minority (most of whom live in Ottawa) for whom Knowlton Nash is an important sex symbol. In other words, our tastes aren't exotic. We like to affect a worldliness about sex, but we blush easily. This doesn't strike me as entirely bad; it may indicate a commendable delicacy of feeling rather than a national streak of prudishness.

Whatever the explanation, none of us were ready for the shocking excesses of Margaret Trudeau — as individuals or as a country. In fact, for a nation that loathes display and reacts to emotional honesty with frosty mistrust, it is hard to imagine a more spectacularly unsuitable political wife. During the late seventies, as her life unravelled in explicit detail before our eyes, an entire people almost died of embarrassment. We didn't know where to look.

Our reactions to Margaret were as intense as they were confused. Curiosity turned to sympathy, then outrage, disgust and, finally, to pity as Margaret talked, danced and shmoozed her way to international notoriety. She must be crazy, we concluded. How else to explain the wild adventures in New York, the impulsiveness, the often hilarious self-delusion. This view had considerable currency among the journalists who covered Maggie. It was succinctly expressed by *Edmonton Journal* writer James Adams in a 1982 column, after he heard a radio interview with Margaret:

In a way that is both hilarious and frightening, the PM's ex showed herself to be the Compleat Flake, stoned on the sound of her own voice, caught in the Woodstock Nation of her mind, unable to see the world on its own terms.

But was Margaret crazy? Was she even unconventional? She certainly cultivated a reckless and wicked style for a while. Like tramp rocker Tina Turner, she became a professional bad girl. But like Tina she was also deeply traditional in her relationships with men, with other women and with the world. She played with the language of feminism, but never really absorbed the message. Her rebellion, in the end, looked more willful and childish than purifying and bold. She chafed against the ludicrous restrictions that bind the life of a political wife as tightly as gauze bound the feet of Chinese women. But Margaret's rebellion was really pretty safe — to everyone but herself. She didn't reject patriarchy, just one particular patriarch. She didn't seriously embrace a feminist future; she never even found a real job. Instead, she found another husband. These days Margaret Trudeau is what she probably always was: a typical, upper middle-class housewife whose time is filled getting and spending, and whose evenings (as far as anyone knows) are spent in New Edinburgh, a quiet red-brick Ottawa neighbourhood that couldn't be farther from Manhattan.

But all that is hindsight. We never really saw Margaret (or Margaret and Pierre, for that matter) clearly. Perhaps we were blinded by her extraordinary beauty — that, and the unexamined prejudices, the unconscious sexism of the time.

In 1971, when Margaret married a fifty-year-old bachelor prime minister who was two years older than her own mother, no one thought she was crazy. Isn't it strange that no one thought he was crazy either — a coldly disciplined intellectual marrying a twenty-two-year-old flower child? What would they talk about over the breakfast table? If he wanted a family why didn't he adopt her? No one asked. For the public, the secret courtship, the clandestine wedding in Vancouver, the photographs of a radiant young woman and a suddenly domesticated Pierre Trudeau conveniently dovetailed with a long-standing romantic fantasy. Remember that Pierre was a national sex symbol at the time. For men, political and economic power have always compensated for an aging body and a receding hairline. Margaret was the classic child bride; breathtakingly beautiful, with a winsome sweetness. The fairytale match was really a very conventional, patriarchal arrangement. It was based on a time-honoured deal: his money and power in return for her youth, beauty and fertility. The fact that youth and beauty tend to be more ephemeral than money and power did not dull the myth.

We didn't know then about Pierre's rigidly organized life, his obsession with physical fitness, his cold control, his aggressive, bullying political personality, his compulsive need to "win" every conversation. All that emerged later. In Linda Griffiths' compelling play, *Maggie and Pierre* the author re-enacts a scene from one of

Margaret's books in which Maggie rips down a prized wall-hanging bearing the slogan that came to summarize Pierre's approach to life, "Reason over Passion." The incident is meant to portray Margaret's wild rage but it tells us as much about Pierre's chilling control.

But in the early days a lot of people looked at the marriage as a vindication of Pierre's sexual and personal power. Nor was anyone shocked by the suggestion that Margaret's chief function was to reflect well on her husband. That was what wives, and particularly political wives, were meant to do. Superficially, the Trudeaus were very contemporary: he was virile despite his age, a fifty-year-old man who could still do effortless back flips, a vital quality in a spouse if ever there was one. Nor did he publicly display the overbearing nature that eventually drove Margaret to reckless rebellion. He appeared to be charmed by his young wife; his obvious awe at her beauty and fecundity could easily be confused for respect for Margaret as a person. Far from behaving like the autocrat that he is, Pierre encouraged his wife to express herself — but on her own time; like many husbands of the time, was he was unwilling to change his own life much to accommodate hers. Seen through a long-distance lens, however, the relationship looked far more appealing than the recurrent, tense negotiations of real marriage.

The union neatly suited Pierre's political needs, too. Now he had a charming hostess, a beautiful political accessory, a public reminder of his virility and power. The marriage put to rest the long-standing questions about his own sexual orientation. (So did Margaret, who once told an interviewer that the suggestion that Pierre was gay was preposterous.) During those first few years, Margaret was the perfect political wife: photogenic, non-intrusive and non-controversial. But none of that came naturally. It never does. Being a political wife is a singularly unnatural state; it is something you have to learn. Some learn more easily than others. Margaret, despite the outward image, was not a quick learner.

Not long after Margaret arrived in Ottawa, she started taking lessons in protocol from the formal, immaculately groomed Mrs. Roland Michener, who conveniently lived right across the road from 24 Sussex at Rideau Hall. Margaret had a lot to learn. It is hard to imagine anyone less suited to the prim ordinariness of life as a political wife than Maggie. She was too young, too informal, too West Coasty, too apolitical for the arcane, dusty social rituals of Ottawa. She wasn't Canada's only hippie, but she was certainly the first to occupy 24 Sussex and, it is a safe bet, the first prime minister's wife to smoke dope in her attic bedroom. She was far more a misfit in official Ottawa than Maureen McTeer, who at least had some professional interest in politics, or Maryon Pearson, whose leisure tastes ran more to British fiction than Studio 54. Unlike McTeer, who spent her teen years immersed in student politics, Margaret rambled around northern Africa wearing "magic sandals" and trying the latest drugs. If she voted at all, it probably would have been for the Green Party.

Margaret was a child of her time, but she was a child in an adult's world, a girl trying to do a lady's job. Canada is strange in this regard: our last three prime ministers' wives — Margaret, Maureen and Mila — have been in their early twenties or thirties, young women trying to function in a job designed for someone much older. We can speculate endlessly about why Canadian prime ministers marry women so much younger than themselves — when they marry at all. After a hard day at Question Period maybe they need someone they can dominate effortlessly at home, although that was hardly the case with Joe and Maureen.

Mrs. Michener, then wife of the governor-general, tried her best to help Margaret. "Protocol will protect you. If you get that right you won't have to put yourself on the line. You'll be judged by your manners," she said. But Margaret never did get it right. In *Beyond Reason*, Margaret recalls that Mrs. Michener (who had been a brilliant academic, herself) told her that when she saw a guest smoking she was to pick up a cigarette herself. When Margaret remonstrated, Michener replied firmly: "Protocol is learning to do all the things that you have to do however much you find them unnatural and trying." What a revealing job description! Unnatural and trying. In hindsight you have to wonder who was crazy.

As for her other wifely duty, Margaret produced two healthy baby boys on subsequent Christmas Days. She was playing that part to perfection. In a patriarchal society everyone loves a madonna. In a 1973 interview, Margaret said:

> As early as I can remember, I longed, longed to be a mother. . . . Certainly I found that pregnancy is just a perfect time in a woman's life, because it is just all happy, positive dreams.

Only the terminally cynical raised eyebrows. The press certainly wasn't cynical.

Early on, Pierre told the media his wife was off limits and the order was respected, except for occasional gushers on the ladies' pages. No one probed the former Margaret Sinclair's past or disturbed her present. On her rare public appearances she looked shy and her uncertainty, along with her exceptional beauty, captivated the press. The official story was that Margaret was deliriously happy behind the gauze curtains at 24 Sussex with her babies (three boys, one after the other) and her tastefully decorated home with its commanding view of the Ottawa River. Who wanted to contradict it? Not Pierre's political contemporaries, who were reassured to see that an older man could still capture a sexy, young woman. Not the Rockcliffe matrons who nodded approvingly every time Margaret had another baby. Everyone had a stake in the fiction, even if it was too perfect to be true.

Living the fiction was something else. Behind the curtains Margaret was finding life trying. She was intimidated by the servants at 24 Sussex at first, and felt like a guest in what was supposed to be her own home. One visitor from those days recalls Margaret walking around a room with a lighted candle to disguise the smell of cigarette smoke, since Pierre forbade smoking in his house. She was uncomfortable and bored in the company of other political wives, most of them old enough to be her mother. In *Beyond Reason*, she describes the lunches she had to give for the wives of visiting delegations: "I sometimes found myself surveying the table with loathing and irritation: what in the world can I possibly find to talk to these crows about?" When she finally emerged from obscurity during the 1972 federal election campaign to join reporters on the press bus, they were stunned — and charmed. "I'm struggling to be myself," she told them. "I'm a mother, I'm a wife, I'm me." Then she went back into seclusion until 1974.

The next time she emerged it was to check herself into the psychiatric ward of a large Montreal hospital, suffering from stress and depression. She handled the personal setback with commendable courage and maturity. "I didn't want to just be caught in the role of politician's wife," she said later.

> I wanted a chance to think about things and to be away from the strains of household and children and just retreat, and it seemed the best way I could do that and get the help that I probably needed, because I was crying a lot, was to seek medical help.

Who could fail to sympathize, or to understand her unhappiness when she said: "I didn't feel sick; I just felt very, very weary and very emotionally tight." In her book, *Beyond Reason*, Margaret filled in the blanks when she revealed that she fled to the hospital to get away from a disintegrating marriage, from cold, hostile silences and from her consuming passion for a prominent American (Ted Kennedy, according to rumours she pointedly refused to deny.)

It was a familiar contemporary story. What made it unusual is that it happened to a political wife. Political wives are not supposed to have breakdowns. What have they go to worry about? They have unlimited expense accounts, maids and nannies; they travel to exotic places, eat at all the best palaces and have national celebrity any time they want it. In fact, the job offers everything but a feeling of self-worth. Margaret Trudeau's experience was a dramatic and sudden indication that something was very wrong — not only with her, but with all the cosy myths about the political wife. But it took us a while to figure that out.

After the breakdown the fairytale rapidly came undone as Margaret started to do peculiar things — peculiar, at least, for political wives. On a trip to Cuba in 1976 she was criticized for wearing jeans and a Liberal party T-shirt on one casual outing. On the same trip she activated ulcers throughout the staid External Affairs Department when she made an unscheduled speech at a reception in Mexico for President Luis Echeverria and his wife, to mark International Women's Year. The department went into deeper shock a few days later, when Margaret rose at an official banquet in Venezuela to sing a ditty she composed for Blanquita Rodriquez de Perez, wife of the Venezuelan president, Carlos Andres Perez.

> I would like to sing to you
> To sing a song of love
> For I have watched you
> With my eyes wide open
> I have watched you with learning eyes. . . .

For official Rockcliffe, the first solid clue that something might be really wrong came one February morning right after the trip, when Margaret actually phoned a private radio talk-show in Ottawa to defend her behavior in Latin America. She was promptly asked to host the show the next week, and did. For a prime minister's wife to appear on radio talk-show — and not even a CBC talk-show — was beyond the pale. If it wasn't specifically prohibited in the political wives' handbook, it is only because such behaviour was unthinkable. (In much the same way, Queen Victoria refused to outlaw lesbianism, on the grounds that it was too fantastic an idea to credit.)

It wasn't until she "ran away" with the Rolling Stones in May 1977, as legend has it, that sympathy towards Margaret Trudeau began to turn to widespread disapproval. What was going on? People were ready to accept and forgive her mental breakdown, but this was different. This looked like willful craziness; this looked like altogether too much fun. Meanwhile, Pierre handled the separation with dignity and an apparent lack of rancour. Overnight, his popularity in the polls rocketed. Hers plummeted. In a custody arrangement that is still unusual in the eighties, he kept the children.

When Margaret started breaking the rules she didn't hold back. She flew to New York, where she danced, drugged, shopped and played at photography. She had sex with actor Jack Nicholson (whom she later described as a "deep, deep soul") in the back seat of his Daimler. She had affairs with Perrier magnate Bruce Nevins and actor Ryan O'Neal. She blabbed her heart out to *Playgirl* magazine and anyone else who would listen. She was used by everyone — Japanese disco owners, magazine editors, celebrity groupies — but she didn't appear to notice or to care. At the nadir of her public disgrace, she was caught by a New York photographer with her pants off. This was Maggie's Tina Turner turn. Like Tina, Margaret seemed to know that her sexually provocative image and slightly wanton style was boffo box office.

The moral absolutists there has never been any mystery about Margaret Trudeau, and her New York adventures merely confirmed the obvious; she was an immature, spoiled brat who dumped her devoted husband and adorable children for a life of easy sex and hard drugs. It is, in fact, still the most serious charge against her. Were the children worried and alarmed by their mother's sudden absences? Were they, as some of Margaret's critics claimed, marked for life? It is impossible to answer those questions without knowing the inner dynamics of the family, but that didn't deter editorialists and column writers.

Well-known British journalist Jean Rook of the *Daily Express*, who was described as "horsey" in one of the Trudeau memoirs, dismissed the prime minister's wife as "a common daisy who will eventually crumble into an autumn maple leaf." Voicing the outrage of many, Rook continued:

> What Margaret has done to her family stinks to high, appalled heaven. To catalogue it in print is to heap manure on insult. Now she lays bare in a grubby book [*Consequences*] things that will mark her children for life.

After that, Ron Collister's comments in the *Edmonton Sun* in March 1982, sound almost kind: "I see a Jekyll and Hyde personality in Margaret Trudeau," he wrote (the crazy theme again). In their interview, he said:

> She was poised, beautiful and friendly, clear-headed and articulate...a pleasure to be with. But *Consequences* is a record of wilfulness, indifference to others, narcissism and self-indulgence. And, in parts, just sleazy.

Through all this it was possible to sympathize with Margaret, to feel a secret exultation that she had sinned so spectacularly against the pious protocols of official life. It was even possible to argue that she had a right to move away from her husband and children for a while to "find herself." Besides, some of her critics were so hypercritical. Yes, Margaret let herself be "used" by some disreputable hustlers and two-bit promoters, but what had Pierre's political handlers been doing? They used her, too. Their exploitation may have been milder, more paternalistic, but it was just as cruel. They wanted her to smile, gush about how wonderful her husband was, look pretty and vague. They didn't want her on her own terms and they were utterly indifferent to what she really thought.

After they recruited her to give a few speeches during the 1974 election campaign, Margaret expected and hoped to play a more active role in politics. She was elated by the warm reception she received and, in a characteristic flight of fancy, imagined herself playing a key role after the election. But she was relegated to the kitchen, expected to become invisible again. It calls to mind a line from a song called "Beast of Burden" by Margaret's pals, the Rolling Stones: "When they're done, they just throw her away."

Even feminists who disapproved of some of the things Margaret did found it hard to align themselves with her critics. There was a waspish tone to many of the articles written about Margaret and, beneath the polished language, the steady hum of sexism. In the august *Spectator*, no less a luminary than Auberon Waugh provided a textbook example of male condescension in an article published in March 1977. "Mrs. T is seen as a typical healthy child of her generation," he drawled.

> Her egotistical ravings are the feminine small talk of innumerable middle class London dinner parties. I have scarcely sat next to a woman in the last ten years who has not told me in the course of the meal, that she is in pursuit of her own self, that she finds the pressure to conform, to do things she doesn't want to do really too much, too much, that her artistic integrity requires greater freedom for its self-expression. Before the meal is over, many of those women are slightly drunk and trying to

pick a quarrel, ending the occasion with an hysterical diatribe about vegetarianism or child care or the best way to educate the lower classes.

In Canada, nationally syndicated columnist Charles Lynch, who was originally smitten with the child bride, oozed sarcasm when he happened upon Margaret's 1979 interview with *Playgirl*. "Mrs. Trudeau visualizes herself speaking at Maple Leaf Gardens, talking about the problems that are really important," he wrote. Lynch obviously doesn't think much of her issues, although he doesn't say why. She told the magazine if she was prime minister she would deal with environmental pollution, disparity towards the Third World, prenatal nutrition, mental retardation, and mental illness. Lynch sneered: "Her political thumbnail sketches are just as penetrating as her policy statements." Lynch was only repeating conventional wisdom: the issues Margaret worried about are still far down on the political agenda. But that doesn't make Margaret the fool.

Margaret made a compelling claim to feminist sympathy, too, when she declared that she would no longer be a rose in her husband's lapel. When she left Pierre in 1977, she told the *Daily Express* she was "abdicating" as the wife of the prime minister, "to take on the more dynamic role of being myself." She added:

> I think if people could see what kind of situation, what kind of life I have had to live for six years, they would understand why I am choosing not to live it anymore. I'm going to devote my time to other interests. They

may be selfish, but I think every woman, every human being, has a right at a certain time in life to be a bit selfish, to be a bit indulgent in their interests.... I hope people will understand. I can't ask them to praise or condemn me. I could only ask them to be tolerant of the fact that the kind of pressures — I mean the pressures on the wives of politicians — is very, very strong. And the pressure to conform, to do certain things that you don't find pleasant, certain things that you find trying, certain things that you find downright insulting to your own personal integrity is really too much. Too much.

It was a theme she continued to sound in the eighties, when she re-established some kind of order in her life. In 1983, in an article she wrote for a Toronto magazine called *PM*, Margaret said that after she left her marriage,

I guiltily assumed there was something wrong with me — that somehow I was at fault for not being happy and fulfilled as a wife. I'm not against marriage and com-mitment. I just could not tolerate an unequal partnership — the old fashioned roles of dominant husband/father, submissive wife/daughter.

She said she wanted to dispel the notion that, "libbers are...men-hating lesbians or disappointed harridans." In 1983 she told one reporter:

I've suddenly realized, to my horror, that I'm a feminist. I never allowed myself to be branded as one, but I can't look away from it, being a working woman and seeing the reality, not the hype and all the ideology of it.

In a quotation worthy of Maureen McTeer, she also declared:

> No one will give us [women] our rights on a silver plat-
> ter. Social change is a continuous process, not absolute.
> Being angry helps — passive resignation and martyrdom
> have no energy potential.

Well, thought a lot of people, it is about time someone said that! Political wifery may be feminism's last frontier, but over the last decade more and more women were starting to notice that the job is intrinsically demeaning. Maybe Margaret would be the first one to "normalize" a ridiculously outdated role. Surely she was entitled to a career as a photographer or an actor or a writer, or whatever she chose to be. Wasn't she right when she complained that the strictures of official life crippled women? Wasn't she brave to defy convention and flee? When they criticized her affairs with Jack Nicholson or Ryan O'Neal or Bruce Nevins, wasn't it the old double standard at work? We didn't hear a whole lot about Jack Kennedy's affairs, although everyone knew he had them. Of course, this all happened before Gary Hart, the man who gave adultery a bad name. But Hart was never criticized in the same way Margaret was: he made an error in "judgment"; she was either crazy or immoral, or both.

Unfortunately, Margaret made life impossible for her defenders. First, there was a mercenary odour to her two tell-all autobiographies (*Beyond Reason*, published in 1979 and *Consequences*, in 1982) — and the unmistakable scent of revenge. She said she only wrote the books because Pierre left her penniless. What was a girl to do? Well, she could have found a job. She could have become a child-care worker — she had a degree in sociology — and learned to live on 15,000 dollars a year. She could have moved in with her wealthy parents for a while. Anything rather than spill the details of her personal life for money. That was not an act of independence, it was living off the avails, and it wasn't only the moral majority who thought so.

Margaret was also quick to abandon sisterhood and resort to pre-feminist behavior when she saw another woman as a rival. She could be catty, mean and personal. After her marriage ended she was visiting the children at 24 Sussex and arrived to find guitarist Liona Boyd's "hideous purple coat" in a downstairs cupboard. She goes on to accuse Pierre's sometime date of being conniving and self-serving. As she wrote, sneeringly, in *Consequences:* "I wasn't surprised when I heard that she called her next album *The First Lady of the Guitar*."

Margaret saved her real vitriol for Maureen McTeer, whom she described in 1979 as, "bouncy, worthy, humourless...a girl from rural Ontario was how I had always seen her, and a keenly ambitious one at that. Intelligent. Very cold." Next to supplanting her, Maureen's real crime in Margaret's eyes was liking blue corduroy. When Joe Clark won the 1979 election and moved into 24 Sussex, Maureen dared to replace Margaret's Fortuny wallcovering with beige paper, then paint the dining room ceiling "a gaudy gold." She replaced Margaret's neutral carpeting with, "the most suburban black and white linoleum." Clark and McTeer left Stornoway, the official residence of the leader of the opposition, "horribly dirty," Margaret writes in *Consequences*, with garbage stacked knee-high in every room. On and on Margaret raves, petty and snide. To her enormous credit, McTeer never rose to the bait.

Most of all, Margaret never made a convincing feminist because of her attitude towards men. It can best be described as worshipful. Men were the centre of her universe, the source of power and approval. Poet Leonard Cohen called her, "every guy's great date." She was always looking for a new guru, for a father, a protector. "I always had a boyfriend, and I would have died if I didn't," Margaret confessed on April 17, 1982. As an adult, she seemed attracted to dominant men who would discipline her, take care of her. She confessed that Pierre, during one particularly heated exchange, hit her. She told a reporter in 1979 about Jean-Luc Fritz, her co-star in the forgettable move *Guardian Angel*: "The thing I love about Jean-Luc is the way he treats me. He doesn't let me get away with a thing. He tells me what to do and doesn't take any of my guff. Besides, he's so handsome."

In *Consequences*, Margaret recalls, without embarrassment, leaping the iron gates to get into Ryan O'Neal's California estate, after he specifically asked her to stay away because he was entertaining his son. In the *Montreal Gazette*, book reviewer Brenda Zosky Proulx tried to be understanding, but finally became utterly exasperated with Margaret's embarrassing narcissism. "So she did it with Jack Nicholson and Ryan O'Neal, " Proulx wrote.

> The only interesting thing about those episodes is that Margaret made it clear how little each of them cared for her. Is it masochism that prompted her to tell us that O'Neal locked her out of his house, or that Nicholson had roses sent to his real girlfriend every day he was with Margaret?

Margaret lashed out against convention, but she was conventional to the core when it came to men.

What finally irritated those inclined to like and support Margaret was her enormous capacity for self-delusion. She seemed to live in a dream world and she was always at the centre of the dream. Despite her talk of being a careerwoman, Margaret only dabbled at various careers — acting, photography, television — and never seemed to have the confidence or discipline to persist. She was extravagant when it came to clothes and household effects, in the tradition of political wives, and her claim that Pierre left her "destitute" when the Trudeaus separated was laughable. "I faced severe poverty as the poorest will face," she told one interviewer.

> Except, fortunately, I am resourceful, educated and re-silient so I was able to overcome it.... I was very much alone, but I was motivated because poverty was unacceptable. I'm not the sort of person who would turn to welfare or unemployment. I don't believe in that unless you are handicapped or mentally sick.

There were protests from low-income groups, one of which picketed the CJOH television studio in Ottawa where Margaret taped her morning interview show, and Margaret apologized for any unintended slight to poor people. But the outburst was typical of a tendency to dramatize her own experiences.

Her books are peppered with literary histrionics. When her marriage faltered, she writes, she flew to Paris in search of Yves Lewis (typically looking to a man for salvation). He was somone she had known in her hippie days and, in her unhappiness, she inflated their brief relationship into a full-blown fantasy. She never found him, but some years later discovered accidentally that he had hanged himself. In *Beyond Reason*, she describes her reaction:

> Being me, the dramatics were spectacular: I pulled my hair, I raved, I screamed, I cried, I refused to believe it. A great emptiness, like a merciless cold wave broke over me.... In the image of Christ to the last, Yves had hanged himself at the age of thirty-three and a half. My search for him is finally over; but unlike Yves I shall go on surviving.

We can only imagine her reaction if someone she knew really well had died.

Margaret saw herself as a tragic heroine at the mercy on an uncomprehending world. She identified with American actress Frances Farmer, who fought a drinking problem and a dominating mother. In *Consequences*, Margaret writes:

> I felt great empathy with Frances Farmer. She had suffered because she was too intelligent and too feminine

and beautiful. I felt the same thing happened in my life.
I knew I had always been too cute for my own good,
too sexy, that I could always get what I wanted and yet
my intelligence forced me to see that it's not enough to
be prom queen. You have to get top marks as well.... I
could see myself as Frances Farmer, or as Saint Joan, or
as any one of the tragic heroines, because I see myself
as a tragic person.

Others saw her as silly. In *Consequences*, Margaret re-
counts the story of her reaction to the defeat of Pierre's
government in 1979. She was in New York and, char-
acteristically, took the news very personally.

I took a bottle of champagne from the fridge and tried
to open it with my teeth, until my friends, who had just
returned, seized it from my mouth. The cork shot off
into the ceiling. A minute more and it would have blasted
into the roof of my mouth. I was too mortified to care.
Then, against all their advice, I insisted on going out to
Studio 54.

Margaret Trudeau, killed in a tragic accident involving
a champagne cork. How apt.

For all that, it is difficult to separate Margaret Trudeau, a sometimes infuriating but not unattractive person, from the role she was meant to play. In the early
days she was too young and too unprepared to be a
feminist hero or a social pioneer, even if she had the
inclination. She was also alone. It takes courage and
persistence to fight the suffocating weight of tradition
in official Ottawa, never mind the weight of her own

husband's disapproval. Trudeau may be the most misogynist prime minister the country has ever had; he certainly held traditional views of women. As Margaret writes and others attest, he put women in airtight categories — the decorative, fellow intellectuals or the functional.

Yet Margaret was not simply a victim of patriarchal oppression or of even the cramped and ludicrous role she had to play. She was too full of odd turns, quirks and caprices to fit anyone's ideological grid. She threw herself with lusty vigour against conventional notions of mother and wife — but in a scattergun, impulsive, indulgent, even self-destructive way. Margaret Trudeau flailed dramatically against the idiocy of being a political wife, but she did the institution no lasting damage. Or, lets hope, herself.

For the last few years she has, in fact, lived a life of exemplary sanity, with her new husband, Century 21 real estate manager Fried Kemper and their son, Kyle, in a leafy Ottawa neighbourhood. She sees Michel, Sasha and Justin, now Montreal schoolboys, on weekends. The only time she makes the newspapers is when she is caught pushing a baby carriage through a nearby park. Soon after Margaret disappeared from the headlines, official Ottawa relaxed its tense muscles and settled back into the old, comfortable routines, little realizing that her successor would be just as shocking, in her own way.

THREE

An unhappy interlude

MAUREEN McTEER AND THE

FOLLY OF FEMINISM

"If I've done anything in redefining what a modern political spouse would be, its simply that I don't pretend not to have any ideas of my own."

MAUREEN McTEER, March 1983

IN ONE OF THE EARLY EPISODES of the venerable "Mary Tyler Moore Show," Mary Richards nervously applies for her first job in television. "You've got a lot of spunk, Mary," Mr. Grant tells her, admiringly. Then there is a pause. "I hate spunk."

Official Ottawa felt much the same way about Maureen McTeer. After madcap Maggie, Maureen was reassuringly sane, serious and self-possessed. She had almost more poise than was natural in a twenty-four-year-old when she emerged from obscurity to "arrive" in Ottawa in June 1976. Unfortunately, she also showed disturbing, early signs of having a mind of her own. This is a seditious quality in a political wife; as history proves, it only leads to grief. The young McTeer — either ignorant or contemptuous of a tradition that only permits a kind of generic niceness from political wives — showed an unbecoming spirit of independence from the beginning.

Unlike Margaret, who anxiously signed up for style lessons soon after she moved into 24 Sussex, Maureen, as wife of the new leader of Her Majesty's Opposition, forged on in law school. Margaret hated official life, but she was too intimidated by it — especially in her first years — to resist. Not Maureen. She made it clear she was too busy to pour tea, too young for horticulture and completely uninterested in the diplomatic hatpin circuit. Because she did not suffer fools gladly, she automatically offended a large constituency in the country's most ambitious village, Rockcliffe Park. But what official Ottawa never got over, and what important segments of the

Progressive Conservative Party still don't accept, is the simple fact that Maureen McTeer kept her own name. Or, as she once tearfully explained, her father's name. Never mind the details, for now. *That* took spunk.

In her own determined, buttoned-down way McTeer attempted nothing short of revolution. She tried to become Canada's first frankly feminist political wife. Because something in her own, flinty personality makes it hard for her to ask for help or cultivate allies, she had to conduct her revolution almost alone. She didn't fail because of anything perverse in her own nature, however, but because of the perversity of the job. A feminist political wife is a contradiction in terms; it is like an impoverished dentist, an impetuous central banker, a taciturn talk-show host. It is like a subtle Joan Rivers. It doesn't exist in nature.

The central belief of feminism, although there are many refinements, is the equality of men and women. But the institution of political wife depends on the "complementarity" of men and women — a sort of different-but-equal gender apartheid favoured by such notable progressives as Carl Jung, Pope Paul II, Phyllis Schlafly and REAL Women. From the time of Agnes Macdonald, the principal function of the political wife has been to sustain, to support, to bolster and, post-Jackie Kennedy, to accessorize her husband. It has not been to lead, to challenge or to go to law school.

Along the way there have been concessions to intellectual fashion. Nowadays a certain plucky spirit and even a post-graduate degree or two is permitted political wives. (In the United States which always leads in these matters, it is almost a prerequisite.) But the wife's primary duty today, as in the past, is to soften her husband's image, to "humanize" him, to embody a sort of Coutts-Hallmark femininity in a Holt-Renfrew label. Maureen was accused of weakening Joe's image, not softening it, as if her square-jawed strength somehow highlighted his essential chinlessness. "I guess the biggest shock to me was all these people saying you cannot have two strong people together — if the woman is strong, the man is weak. The reality is that to have a strong woman, you need a very strong man," Maureen said in 1982. It may be reality, but as she and Joe found out, it is also bad politics.

The richest irony is that, stripped to its essence, there is nothing in McTeer's curriculum vitae that REAL Women could object to. She was close to her family and particularly to her father, John McTeer, a modestly-paid government employee and farmer who took his daughter to her first political meeting when she was twelve. She was brought up conventionally, the second of six children, on a farm in Cumberland, Ontario, thirty kilometres from Ottawa. It was from her father and her family that the Roman Catholic McTeer learned an almost Protestant sense of social responsibility. She told Charles Lynch that John McTeer, who died in 1978, taught her,

> that I have a responsibility, because I was fortunate enough, not just to be born in a democracy — and this may sound Pollyanna and idealistic — but because I was

given an education and, fortunately, was born with a brain.

McTeer did pursue an education, but she also married, at the relatively young age of twenty-one, a man thirteen years her senior. She put her own career on hold twice to help Joe in his political climb. She had a cute, apple-cheeked daughter named Catherine, baked an expert farm pie and dressed like a lady. Dressed, at times, like a minor member of the royal family. That oracle of orthodoxy, Zena Cherry, the *Globe and Mail* society columnist, even praised Maureen for her Canadian labels and her impeccable style.

Nor could Maureen be accused of being anti-family, which is the right's enduring slander against feminism. During the terrible days of 1979 and 1980, Maureen stood by her man, as steadfast as Pat Nixon. "I've done more than any spouse in the world, Rosalynn Carter excepted, to ensure support for my husband because it is very lonely in that role," she said in January 1984. It was true. She suffered with her husband and for him.

Maureen did write a book, but it was a chatty, kindly book — not on feminist theory but on official residences, an inventory of the nooks, crannies, carpets and wall-mouldings of the famous. (Of the spiral staircase at 24 Sussex, she wrote: "It certainly does seem to be a staircase made for a bride's elegant pose.") What could be more wifely than that? Decorating, after all, is the political wife's first duty and Maureen was never one to turn her back on duty. Not only that, her own style was middle class, modest and functional, and not at all wild and worldly — the style of the perfect daughter-in-law.

Margaret Trudeau hated it. When Joe and Maureen moved into 24 Sussex in 1979, Margaret complained loudly that an era of elegant brocade was being swept away on a proletarian wave of blue corduroy. Undaunted, Maureen recycled carpets she found in the basement of Rideau Hall. She and Joe didn't share Margaret's personal habits or big city appetites, either. They drank coke, they didn't snort it. They were out to "deglamorize" the top job, in Maureen's words. They were immediately labelled hicks by certain liberal sophisticates, and that alone should have endeared them to traditionalists. In a snide 1979 piece in *Chatelaine* magazine, journalist Sean Rossiter pointed out that Maureen had seen the movie *Rocky* three times, while Joe saw it once. Rossiter remarked, acidly: "As pressure builds, McTeer and Clark will take little solace in the rich, cultural background that has sustained great leaders in times of stress." But all that was fine with REAL Women and others nostalgic for a Reaganite, small-town yesterday that probably never existed.

Best of all, Maureen was a conservative. It may not mean much on Ottawa's spongy, non-ideological political terrain but to the Christian, anti-feminist right it sure beat "liberal." In fact, Maureen McTeer could have been REAL Women's dream candidate for First Lady, except for the inconvenient matter of her (shudder) feminism.

Unlike Margaret, Maureen didn't adopt feminism as a political "look" when she entered public life. Her feminism, which was more a strong sense of self than an ideology in the early days, predated her life in the lime-light and was not just a phase or an intellectual pose. Her personal history suggests it was almost a facet of her personality. With Margaret, feminism was a style, something she apparently picked up in New York, something that gave her a certain intellectual cachet in some circles for a time. But it made no lasting impression. Margaret left her marriage not to strike out on her own, but to find another man. She did. In fact, she found a number of them. Throughout her period in the public eye, Margaret always looked to men for approval no matter how liberated she sounded, whereas Maureen didn't appear to look to anyone for anything.

When she was in her late teens Maureen was invited to enter a Young Progressive Conservative beauty contest. "I was so outraged at the idea, that I ran for the executive of the association on an anti-beauty contest platform, and I was elected," she told an interviewer in 1976. "The YPCs don't have beauty contests any more." In college, McTeer recalls going to a New Democratic Party convention with a school friend when she was eighteen or nineteen, only to find women's issues being "laughed at." (The whole experience apparently turned her off the NDP for life.) She fought for feminist causes at law school and was a founder of the University of Ottawa's women-in-law caucus.

When she entered public life, Maureen signalled, in many small ways, that she was not about to trot obe-diently behind her husband in the heel position recommended for political spouses. At the 1976 convention that chose Joe Clark party leader, she was the only wife to go to the stage with her husband when he gave his crucial speech. "I believe men and women are equal and I will fight to the death anyone who proposes legislation or programs or policies, in any political party, that will deny women that," she told journalist Charles Lynch in 1983. It is probably as good a summary as any of McTeer's animating belief.

The problem is that half the country didn't like it and the other half didn't believe it. In the black, macho heart of the Ottawa Press Club, Maureen was often as not described as a ball buster. Part of the deep contempt for Joe Clark in the gallery sprang from the notion that, as one journalist wrote, Maureen ran him "like a toy truck." Some early stories about her were etched in acid, redolent of all the tired stereotypes about castrating bitches and henpecked husbands. One memorably cruel cartoon in the *Ottawa Citizen* showed a butchy looking Maureen riding horseback on a goofy looking Joe. In the *Saint John Evening Telegraph*, columnist Ken Chisholm wrote ten years ago:

> Apart from the fact that I think this Ms. business is a lot of damn nonsense, to me it does not appear very smart politically for a national party leader to be running around the country with a Ms. tucked under his arm. That might impress the kooks, but it won't be the kooks who elect the government.

He concluded: "Margaret may do some strange things at times, but at least we always know she is Mrs. Pierre

Trudeau, wife of the prime minister." Isn't it interesting that he considered Maureen's feminist gesture of keeping her name more threatening than Margaret's highly publicized sexual infidelity? Perhaps he figured that Margaret, at least, liked men. With Maureen he wasn't quite sure.

I am convinced that it was Maureen's feminism that scared men like Chisholm — and other less outspoken critics — and not her personality. She is, after all, probably no more intelligent, ambitious or self-possessed than Mila Mulroney. Yet Mila is the perfect political wife by traditional male standards; she doesn't threaten men, she comforts them. That may be because Mila's energy and intelligence are directed exclusively towards helping her husband; she uses her gifts in the service of a man and, by extension, of all men. She doesn't appear to have or want a relationship with the broader world; family is her only frame of reference. Maureen, on the other hand, has a range of personal interests and opinions — not to mention an independent career. Some of her views overlap with Joe's but she doesn't necessarily reflect his every thought. Mila is a mirror of her husband, repeating, with sweet reasonableness, every campaign slogan and political cliché, but Maureen has always sent out light from her own source.

These distinctions were lost on Maureen's critics. In Rossiter's cutting *Chatelaine* profile he writes that McTeer demanded to know why the magazine had sent a man to do the interview (quite a legitimate question), then took him horseback riding at the family farm in Cumberland, hoping he would fall. As he wrote: "When she feels superior, she is Nightingale McTeer, comforter of wounded sparrows. To anyone who might be competition, she is Hammerlock McTeer, tough customer."

When her habitual control occasionally snapped and she "wept openly" as the press loves to say, her chauvinist critics could barely contain their glee. In Winnipeg, during the 1980 winter campaign, exhausted from travel and law exams, McTeer burst into tears at a high-school rally when a young woman asked her why she kept her own name. That familiar, taunting question coming from a young woman was more than McTeer could bear. As she explained later:

> As I spoke to her my Irish temper got the best of me because she had challenged not just me, but all women, and she had forgotten by her question that we are all links in a great chain.

A tearful McTeer later explained that she and her father were very close, "and I keep my name because I'm proud of my name." She felt obliged to explain that for women who do the same, it "in no way detracts from the love of their husbands." The *Montreal Gazette* headline trumpeted: "Its Ms. McTear." Ah-hah! She cried! She's a woman after all.

In 1983, McTeer remarked with justification, that,

> When I said I was a feminist, all those pack journalists assumed that meant that any qualities our society has defined as feminine, such as sensitivity or caring for

people, were automatically negated. I suffered because
I was perceived as too masculine, and Joe suffered because
he showed he cared for others and was too feminine.

Some were quick to blame McTeer's image problems
not on her feminism, but on her "difficult" personality.
That is a loaded adjective for feminists, strident and
otherwise. Had Maureen been a man she might have
been described as "forceful" rather than "difficult." As
McTeer herself pointed out in 1976: "The words *ambitious* and *aggressive* are often used pejoratively when
they are applied to women." But sexism aside, McTeer
was an intense, partisan and often prickly person. Her
sense of humour could be heavy-handed and sarcastic;
it probably hurt as many people as it amused.

Like a lot of self-styled tough customers, McTeer also
avoided easy intimacy. Except with a few close friends,
Moe, as she was known, was guarded and fiercely private. Few people realized that she suffered from migraine headaches most of her life or that the prospect of
publicity — an interview or a photo session — could
completely unnerve her. In 1983 she talked to journalist
Charles Lynch about living with tension:

I don't remember a time in my life when there wasn't
some tension. Either the weather was bad and the crop
wasn't going to be good enough, or there wasn't enough
for Christmas, or someone was sick, or someone had
died. There's always tension in life.

She was especially worried about the security of her
family and was physically ill when the Pope was shot.

In *Residences* she writes: "People can live with the loss of privacy. But I, for one, am not sure I will ever be able to live with the knowledge that my loved ones are never secure."

Maureen hid that anxiety and doubt in public. It may have been her rural conservative roots or a family tradition of privacy about personal matters. Whatever, it was deeply ingrained. "One of the problems [in public life] is that people really do think they can form immediate, deep personal links with you," she complained in a 1982 interview. There would be no soul-baring for McTeer. "It has always been a discouragement to people that I don't break down and cry," she told Adele Freedman in a revealing interview in the *Globe and Mail*, also in 1982.

> It is very fashionable to pour your heart out now, in public especially, because then you get more play. I've always believed there's part of you that's private and that you should keep it private. I also believe people see through phonies.

(She wasn't specifically referring to Mila, but she could have been.)

> It's one of my real strengths and real weaknesses, at the same time, that I am completely unable to be a hypocrite. If I don't like you, I don't like you — and that's a very great disadvantage in public life.

It was. Political wives, after all, are supposed to be marketing certain female qualities: compassion, warmth, good humour. Maureen's self-possession was often mistaken for coldness and sometimes it was no mistake. While Joe seemed to exorcise his anger or bury it deep inside, McTeer bristled as her husband's long, public humiliation continued. In a 1986 interview Clark said he was glad Maureen was now practising law and living her own life; the fishbowl existence was far harder on her nerves than his.

For her part, she mistrusted the press, the party and anyone she didn't know. In 1984 she told the *Toronto Star* that after Joe lost power after only seven months, certain Tories, "did everything possible to make Joe look weak. There were constant plots. It's a little like a cancer — you're never sure where it's coming at you from." It is easy to see why Maureen would feel wary. But that wariness made it hard for people to warm to her. She had sympathizers — even in official Ottawa — but she didn't trust easily.

At least she wouldn't, like Margaret, be blurting out her intimate secrets at state dinners, inducing spasms of disgust in distinguished British misogynists like Auberon Waugh. Not that Waugh or anyone of a similarly sexist bent would prefer Ms. McTeer as a dinner companion. She wasn't inane, flighty or self-indulgent the way Margaret occasionally was. Quite the opposite. She was serious, high-minded and not easily impressed. Waugh would no doubt have found Maureen tiresomely prosaic and sullen. He would have complained — in a phrase that will ring alarm bells in every feminist ear — that she had an "attitude problem." Political wives must constantly walk a narrow line; they have to please men without being too pleasing, flatter them without being too transparent and entertain them without being too provocative. Who can blame Maureen for not playing a game that no wife can win?

Of course official Ottawa — the high-income politicians, bureaucrats and judges who work on Parliament Hill and sleep in Rockcliffe, and remain largely impervious to faddish social upheavals like feminism — isn't the whole country. It just thinks it is; call it delusions of langour. In universities and elsewhere in the mid-seventies there were other young women like McTeer, intrigued by Simone de Beauvoir, *Ms.* magazine and the rise of US liberal feminism. There were even a few men like Joe Clark, invigorated rather than frightened by the rising of the women. Why weren't they defending and supporting Maureen in the critical early years when the Tory party's George Hees faction was after her hide?

Well, for one thing, anyone with a progressive turn of mind wasn't (and isn't) likely to look to Parliament Hill for role models. On top of that, the very notion of an avowed Progressive Conservative being a feminist was enough to provoke hilarious disbelief in some circles. In other circles, McTeer was ahead of her time. "I had quite a bad image for a long time," she told the *Globe and Mail* in 1985, "but if you're Panasonic, a little ahead of your time, sooner or later public opinion is going to catch up." It was later rather than sooner. Feminism was no longer a fringe activity in 1976, but it still made a lot of people nervous — particularly McTeer's unapologetic, undiluted brand of feminism. If many women her age secretly admired Maureen, most lacked her blunt courage. Strong women frighten people — men and women — in a way that strong men don't. Maybe their obvious vitality demolishes the myth of the natural subservience of women, a myth both men and women have sheltered in. Whatever the reason, not everyone wanted to be identified with feminism or with McTeer, whose strength of conviction was matched by a commanding physical presence, an unbending carriage and strong, no-nonsense features.

It is fortunate that McTeer was strong, because she was very much alone when she first arrived in official Ottawa. She later confessed that the brief period when Joe was prime minister in 1979, and she was a twenty-seven-year-old mother and law student, was one of the loneliest of her life. It wasn't much better when she was living in Stornoway, the square-shouldered stucco mansion the taxpayers provide for the leader of the opposition. Her first revolutionary act was serving raw vegetables at an official reception, a year before crudités became fashionable in official Ottawa. *Quelle scandale!* While her contemporaries were taking back the night, or cramming for exams, or dashing off to consciousness-raising groups, Maureen was trying to revolutionize the grazing habits of the privileged. A fruitless task if ever there was one.

She didn't get much support from the feminist left, either. In academic feminist strongholds and in feminist organizations and magazines, McTeer ran right into a deep, almost visceral suspicion of conservatives. The Phyllis Schlaflys might appropriate some feminist language, but everyone knows where their true interests lie: with the patriarchal power system that sustains them. But to compare McTeer's conservatism to Schlafly's betrays a deep ignorance of both women, and of the enormous differences between Canadian and US politics.

The brand of conservatism McTeer espouses is a gentle, northern variant of the rigorous, right-wing Reaganism that is on the rampage down south. McTeer, like Flora MacDonald, David Crombie and Joe Clark, is a Red Tory. Red Tories can be ferociously anti-Soviet and as blindly enthusiastic about "free" enterprise as the Reaganites. But on matters of personal justice they subscribe to a mild, United Church style conservatism that is far too mannerly and civilized to permit the blatant oppression of one gender or class or race, by another. They accept the claims of feminism, even though they usually prefer remedies so gradual as to be totally ineffectual. Red Tories don't seek to uproot patriarchy for once and for all — they generally shudder at the prospect of cataclysm or revolution — but they try to ameliorate its excesses.

This kind of conservatism has been called "moderate" and "Canadian" and "decent" but these are value-laden adjectives. Moderate compared to what? Decent towards whom? It certainly hasn't made any dent in the wage gap between men and women. It hasn't attacked the feminization of poverty. Its headiest achievement is the appointment of a few women to the Senate and the

Supreme Court. Perhaps Canadian conservatism — elements of which are found in the Liberal and New Democratic Party, too — is as fundamentally incompatible with giving women an equal share of power as the more virulent American strain. But it definitely isn't as hateful.

We should also beware of assuming that Tories are necessarily worse than Liberals or New Democrats when it comes to attitudes towards women. It is true that party demographics show a higher-than-normal number of Colonel Blimps and Mister Blusters in Tory ranks. But when it comes to exercising power, all the male-dominated, mainstream parties appear content to relegate women's issues, or justice issues (which is what they really are) far down the political agenda, somewhere after hog-pricing policy. The New Democrats have more progressive rhetoric but any real differences in the way they treat women are not readily visible to the naked eye. And the Liberals under Pierre Trudeau or John Turner are certainly no more friendly to feminism than the Tories were under Joe Clark. (Even as external affairs minister, Clark continues to insist on seeing women's names when he scans lists for promotion.)

So the purity of Maureen's feminism doesn't have much to do with whether or not she calls herself a Tory. In fact, by Ottawa's pathetically inadequate standards, Maureen McTeer and Joe Clark are as feminist as it gets — even if they are conservative.

While McTeer's feminism was far from decorative, in a crunch she could put party solidarity ahead of sisterhood, just like any other mainstream politician. Some say it happened on February 14, 1981 when about one thousand women flocked to Ottawa for an historic, ad-hoc meeting on women and the Constitution. Maureen and a group of Tory women, including Flora Mac-Donald, were trying to convince the group to pass a resolution opposing Trudeau's plan for unilateral repatriation of the Constitution — the line Joe Clark was pushing in the Commons. However other feminists on Parliament Hill that day, many of them New Democrats, wanted an addition to the Charter of Rights guaranteeing equal treatment for men and women. They were more interested in getting a Canadian version of the E.R.A. than in the niceties of constitutional prøcedure. McTeer stood at a microphone for twenty minutes without being acknowledged, then stormed out of the room in angry tears. She complained later that NDP and Liberal women railroaded the meeting. But some participants said Maureen's purpose was to score points for the Tories, not win rights for women.

Other feminists, initially pleased when McTeer kept her name, became cynical later when her protectors tried to explain she had done it, not as a means of self-assertion, certainly not as an insult to her husband, but to honour her father. This may have been protective covering, and God knows she needed it in the early days. But there has always been an unseemly rush on the part of some of her friends to downplay the feminist nature of her decision, to take the sting out of what has since become a commonplace custom. In 1986, *Maclean's* magazine quoted her law colleague, Jeff Lyons, as saying that

Maureen kept her family name out of respect for her father, not lack of respect for her husband. Lyons continued: "She always says to me that he [Joe] is the boss, and I believe her." The implication is clear; there, there, she isn't really a feminist tyrant after all. It was all just a misunderstanding.

There is an apologetic note in all this, which feeds the canard that feminism is anti-men — that keeping your name is a hostile rather than affirmative act. Feminism doesn't hate men; it deplores patriarchy. Feminists aren't hostile to all males, but to patriarchal behavior in men and institutions. These may seem trivial distinctions, but they aren't. The fact that they still have to be spelled out shows that we haven't come such a long way, Baby.

The farther Maureen moves from the centre of political power the more free she is to be feminist, within strict limits. In recent years, now that Joe is in no apparent danger of becoming prime minister again, Maureen's speeches have been more pointed; she has spoken in favour of mandatory affirmative-action programs, warned against writing health policy based on an outdated concept of the two-parent nuclear family and said the greatest hypocrisy is the charge that feminists are anti-family. She has taken up the cause of female victims of the microchip, arguing that women must learn to use technology, not be displaced by it.

Maureen took her most breathtaking political risk in 1986 when she spoke out on abortion. At thirty-four years old, fully conscious of the consequences of her action, she marched right into the most intractable, ugly debate of them all. When summoned by her bishop, Adolophe Proulx of Hull, to give an accounting of herself for accepting a position on the board of the Canadian Abortion Rights Action League (CARAL), she said publicly that she wouldn't have an abortion but, "as a lawyer, a mother and a Christian" she believed every woman has the right to control her own fertility. She hoped her stand would send a "positive signal" to Roman Catholic women who don't agree with the Church's stand.

"I find it rather amusing that the pro-abortionists would find this a coup," sniffed right-to-lifer Laura McCarthur. "Who cares? Who is she? Who even remembers her? I think she is a person who is some kind of hang-over from the flower-child age." McCarthur concluded: "It's a pity. She would have had such great impact as the first lady of Canada if she had taken herself away from the flower children she has united with."

Flower children? In the Tory backrooms? Doubtful, but never mind. By 1986 it was McCarthur, not McTeer, who was crying in the wilderness. Public opinion had caught up with Joe Clark's audacious wife at last. Press reaction to her stand on abortion was respectful, supportive. When Christian anti-abortion crusader Kenneth Campbell wrote Prime Minister Mulroney, accusing Maureen of bringing "shame on the government and the nation who honoured her husband," and demanding that Joe Clark resign his cabinet post, there was incredulity. The *Regina Leader Post* said the idea of Clark resigning was "ludicrous and insulting." The *Vancouver Province* called the notion "a throwback to darker days."

Even the staid *Globe and Mail* remarked that Campbell's letter would elicit "a puzzled silence in many Canadian households. Followed by unrestrained laughter." The rabidly right-wing *Toronto Sun* supported Maureen, calling Campbell and his like "moral bullies."

The drama led Tory guru Dalton Camp to muse on Maureen's unique role in Canadian public life:

> She became the first wife of a prominent public man who was also, it soon became clear, someone else. This sort of thing takes getting used to, especially in politics, where so much is symbolic and role-playing is not just a game, but the only game. Politicians wives, like their spouses, are public property, and not even Jackie Kennedy asked to be called Jackie Bouvier.

In her *Toronto Sun* column, the peppery Laura Sabia proclaimed: "The days of the dutiful wives of prominent men, with eyes upturned in simulated admiration, are gone forever."

Not so fast, Laura. Maureen's eyes may not be upturned, but her lip is still buttoned, and will be as long as her husband plays a prominent role in politics. She writes a monthly column in *Chatelaine* that is a perfect illustration of the limits on her freedom. The column is careful, dull and dutifully respectful of government. It isn't propaganda, but it isn't journalism either. It is more in the nature of a regular public service announcement. She fills us in on the latest, daring Senate appointments; the latest collection of promises from the latest government report. One thing she dares not do is criticize Brian Mulroney. He is not only prime minister, he is her husband's boss. Brian doesn't like to be "blindsided," and he is not above punishing Joe for Maureen's misdeeds. Abortion is a tricky subject, but it can also be regarded as a personal, moral issue which transcends petty partisanship. Besides, Maureen's position is not out of line with majority opinion in this country.

But things would get very tricky indeed, were she to criticize the government's employment equity legislation, for instance, or its failure to live up to any number of campaign promises to women. It leaves McTeer hopelessly compromised — an apologist for a government whose notion of feminism can be charitably described as undeveloped, and press agent for a man who betrayed and undermined her husband and who doesn't have a feminist bone in his body. No wonder some accuse McTeer of being a toy feminist, writing a toy column. It didn't help her case when the Canadian Press reported that she was using a woman in Joe's office to research her *Chatelaine* pieces for her. (The woman later said she was being paid by Maureen for the work.)

Of course, Maureen won't really be free until she runs for office herself, thereby giving the words *political wife* a whole new meaning. If she wants justice for women, she's going to have to fight for it openly, not plead for it from the sidelines. As this book was being written, Maureen was considering running for the Tories in an Ottawa-area seat during the next federal election. If she runs and wins, she will be pioneering again: Joe and

Maureen could become the first husband-and-wife team to sit in the Commons as members of Parliament at the same time. What a fascinating prospect.

She would be no freer, however, to criticize Brian Mulroney than she is now. But having her own seat in Parliament would give her a legitimacy, a clout that no political wife, however accomplished, will ever possess. It would probably be deeply satisfying to Maureen, too, to be finally judged on her accomplishment rather than her style. There is no doubt she would make a diligent MP, a woman who is home at last.

Not that we should exaggerate the power of the individual MP, or even cabinet minister, to advance the cause of women in Ottawa. Mulroney has three strong women in his cabinet — Barbara McDougall, Pat Carney and Flora MacDonald. But all are, in one way or another, peripheral to the real power. Flora is off in a side pocket, in the little-noticed communications ministry. Carney has the important trade portfolio ("Pat has the ball, now watch her run with it"), but that has looked like a setup from the beginning. If the free trade talks with the United States fail, Carney gets the blame. If they succeed, Brian gets the credit. McDougall, a very tough and cool political operative, has the relatively minor privatization portfolio, along with responsibility for status of women. After her brilliant defence of the government during the 1985 bank failures, McDougall was earmarked for bigger things. However Mulroney, unaccountably, gave her two relatively junior jobs. His defenders claimed by putting a proven performer like McDougall into the women's portfolio, he was elevating its importance. However he didn't increase the budget or make any specific commitments to women.

The McDougall appointment was more likely another example of the stunning insensitivity (blindness, really) that has always marked Brian's approach to women as a political force. He first gave the status-of-women job to Walter McLean, an ineffectual Presbyterian minister from Waterloo who spent most of his time checking over his shoulder to make sure his job was secure. Then, Brian chose McDougall, an individualist with no particular sympathy for feminism. Would Mulroney dare give the women's portfolio to Maureen McTeer? Wouldn't it be ironic if that became the acid test of his commitment to gender equality?

If Maureen McTeer's experience proves anything it is that political wife is simply not a respectable job, no matter how respectable the incumbent. It is bestowed, not earned. It is either volunteerism to the max, or a very classy sort of escort service. It is an affront to the merit principle. To those who believe political wives should be gracious and largely silent, McTeer's opinions on such matters as abortion are not only unwelcome, but unprofessional. (No one has yet accused Mila Mulroney, for example, of being unprofessional.) To those who believe in representational democracy, unelected political wives have no right to taxpayer-funded offices, no place at the cabinet table and no authority to take part in public debates. So Maureen lives quietly in Ottawa, dabbles at law, public speaking and journalism and waits for parole.

It should be written somewhere in the job description for political wife, "feminists need not apply." Not that it would have saved Maureen McTeer much grief. After all, it isn't a job you apply for; it is a job you marry into. Once there, McTeer tried to find a compromise between her own beliefs and the essential weightlessness of the job. She failed to reform the institution of political wife, just as Margaret Trudeau failed to subvert it. Critics say McTeer didn't try hard enough; that for all her brave talk she was the real wimp in the family. More charitable observers believe Maureen was a pioneer, that she broke ground for the women to follow. But look who followed.

Maureen is even more constrained on the subject of Mila than she is about Brian. But her heart must have descended to the snub toes of her Italian leather shoes as she watched Mila efficiently turn back the clocks all over Ottawa. In 1985 Maureen made some careful remarks to a reporter, to the effect that if Mila was the only role model available to women that might be a problem; but that among the plethora of images around today Mila represents only one option.

It is an option official Ottawa loves. Spunk, but no surprises. When Mila Mulroney moved into power and Maureen McTeer moved out, the sigh of relief blew out leaded-glass windows all over Rockcliffe. At a private party shortly after he took office, Mulroney confided to a few guests that he was apprehensive about how Ottawa and the country would receive the very traditional Mila, after the frankly feminist Maureen. Whatever the country may have thought, the Tory party loved Brian's wife. Not long after she arrived in Ottawa, Mila laughingly assured a group of Tories that she had no plans to start using her own name. "With a name like Pivnicki, do you blame me?" She was charming. So much nicer than that caustic Ms. McTeer.

FOUR

Shopping your way to the top

MILA MULRONEY AND THE TRIUMPH

OF APPEARANCE OVER

ACCOMPLISHMENT

"I know my role and I know my limitations. What I do within those limitations, that's up to me. I have always been very much accountable for everything I say."

MILA MULRONEY, March 1986

WITH MILA MULRONEY, THE NOSE is the mirror of the soul. In fact, it is amazing how many people have formed an impression of Mila based on her nose or, to be specific, on the way she crinkles her nose. It has become her trademark, that and the automatic smile, the careless tossing of the chestnut hair, the explosion of noisy delight when she spots someone she knows, however slightly, in a crowd. Mila *works* a crowd, silky and insincere as any political pro, drawing people to her with her long, slender arms for a perfunctory embrace, always keeping one eye on the nearby television cameras. She is like the beauty contest winners who practise their expressions of joy and wild surprise for hours in the privacy of their New York City hotel rooms, so they can totally abandon themselves to emotion at the moment of victory — without ruining their mascara. There is something patently insincere about Mila, something people can sense, even through a television screen.

She never lets down her guard in public, never gives us a glimpse of what really irritates, amuses or pleases her. She would have us believe that she lives in a world with no rough edges, sudden failings or crude power grabs, that she and her husband are committed only and always to "Brian's dream for Canada." Her speeches are clichés-on-a-string, more platitudinous, if that is possible, than her husband's. She substitutes euphemism for conversation; she once told a reporter, in all seriousness, that Brian is "sensitive" rather than "thin skinned."

Other wives, in various ways, have winked sardon-
ically at the rest of us, indirectly acknowledging that
they know how phoney the job of political wife can be,
how phoney politics can be, and that *they* know that *we*
know. Maryon Pearson used her acerbic wit and Maureen McTeer her forthright personality to express their
reservations about the life of the political wife. It is
obvious, too, that Geills Turner is ambivalent about the
role, not so much by anything she says as by her terse-
ness, her volatility. Even Nancy Reagan is opening up
slightly as she nears the end of her reign, denouncing
criticism of her meddling in White House affairs as "silly."
Not Mila. In the rare interviews she gives (men reporters
are preferred) she disgorges banal observations and vague
good intentions with the same passion that goes into a
computer printout. She never varies her script.

In the beginning the script was popular, at least in
Tory circles. Mila was everything a political wife should
be: bright, attractive, well dressed and entirely devoted
to her husband's career. During the '84 campaign, Mila
was Brian's greatest (critics said only) political asset.
Fashionable and photogenic, she was a relief to traditional Tories — especially after Maureen McTeer, with
her steely reserve and dangerous notions. Mila didn't
simply tolerate campaigning, she loved it. She knew her
place, too; it was beside (and slightly behind) her husband on a political platform, not sweating out a bar exam
in another city. "Liberated" men found Mila warm and
non-threatening, yet intelligent enough to meet their
exacting, new standards. For an older generation she

was a vindication; after feminism's uncomfortable questions, Mila was living evidence that certain truths about
men and women (and their relative power) endure.

The media, with some commendable exceptions, was
smitten. *Chatelaine* magazine declared Mila Woman of
the Year in 1986, as feminists across the country gagged.
The old power-behind-the-throne story re-emerged,
dressed (by Creeds) in the style of the eighties. "Una-
bashed wife and mother," heralded *Chatelaine*, adding
in breathless qualification: "She's both, of course,
exuberantly so, but she's also an equal partner in a high-
powered marriage, and a working mother with a schedule
that never lets up." For every article that questioned
Mila's political "interference," or reported that she had
asked her Mountie guards to salute her, there were five
others describing the joy she brought to an old folks'
home. She was a bracing corrective to all those dreary
tracts that some magazines (even *Chatelaine*) used to
publish about the oppression of women. In short, Mila
embodied a bunch of notions that became unfashionable
in the seventies, but are so central to male privilege they
never really died.

By the late eighties the script was wearing thin. Feminism has changed public expectations of a political wife
since the days of Olive Diefenbaker — even if those
changes still haven't penetrated the heart of power, or
the mind of the Tory party. For a lot of people there is
something distasteful about the way that Mila is content
to be a passenger on her husband's ambition, the way
she pretends to be less than she is — less accomplished,

less astute, less ambitious — the way she exercises power covertly. The stories about the hundred-dollar-a-roll wallpaper and Mila's runaway consumerism fed the dis-illusionment; there was a general mistrust of Mila, a sense that she was pretending to be someone she wasn't, that she was putting something over on all of us.

It was becoming increasingly obvious that, all things being equal, Mila would rather be shopping. *Toronto Sun* columnist Claire Hoy started referring to the Mulroneys as Mr. Pomp and Mrs. Circumstance. It seemed that, left to her own devices, Mila would kiss Canada good-bye in an instant, move to West Palm Beach and devote herself entirely to travel, gracious dining and home ren-ovations. Former *Saturday Night* editor Robert Fulford once wrote:

> Like royalty, First Ladies draw their power and fame not from personal accomplishment but from family con-nections. This gives them, as it gives royalty, the ability to transcend ordinary political debate and do for their subjects what constitutional monarchs do for theirs; em-body ideals of virtue, legitimize public events by their presence, bring a sense of grace to otherwise common-place institutions, and act as celebrities whose lives their citizens vicariously enjoy.

Mila obviously enjoyed acting as a celebrity, but she was not good at embodying "ideals of virtue." She made desultory stabs at doing good, but seemed to lack the sense of public service that the Royal Family, Eleanor Roosevelt, even Nancy Reagan, have brought to their jobs. She made much of her ethnic background — she was born in Yugoslavia and emigrated to Canada when she was five — but she didn't involve herself in the problems of most concern to ethnic communities, refugee and immigration policy. She was interested in the arts and at one time considered becoming an architect but, unlike Maryon Pearson, for example, she did not take on the role of patron for Canadian artists. Nor did she have Maureen McTeer's desire to change things or to escape the life of political wife for something better. Mila left and leaves the unshakable impression that her chief political and social goal is hanging on to the perks and privileges of public life. It is as if she has one mantra: get reelected. All along there had been hints of an imperious nature, an astonishing appetite for things, but these traits didn't really surface until 1987.

On a dreary, windy day in April, Mila Mulroney and Nancy Reagan were cosily ensconced inside the National Arts Centre in Ottawa, at an elegant luncheon that hardly anyone knew about. Hardly anyone unimportant, that is. It was a strictly private affair for ninety special guests — a "cross-section of Canadians" officials said later, which included National Capital Commission chairman Jean Pigott, newspaper columnist Charlie Lynch, teen model Monika Schnarre, national sex symbol Knowlton Nash and Mila's hairdresser, Rinaldo Conancio. The guests nibbled filet supreme of pheasant stuffed with wild mushrooms, Manitoba perch with Atlantic salmon *mignonnettes*, spring salad, julienned vegetables and poached Fiorelli pears and sabayon, in a room decorated with tulips and fresh spring flowers. A designer menu, with a designer musical ensemble known as Sidewalk Bach tinkling discreetly in a corner. In a brief speech, Mila described Nancy as Canada's best friend, and Nancy, who was reportedly seated between Brit cartoonist Ben Wicks and Swiss-born shoe magnate Sonya Bata, said nothing. All the men, according to one guest, were watching Schnarre.

If it wasn't for the obsessive pursuit of the trivial for which Parliamentary Press Gallery reporters like myself are so justly famous, even these meagre details would never have emerged. Curiously, the luncheon didn't appear on the exhaustively detailed itineraries handed out to the hundreds of journalists who covered the Reagan-Mulroney summit that April. Ordinarily, such events are scripted to the smallest detail, with little agendaettes for the wives. Luncheons like the one I am describing are major photo opportunities for serious first ladies, their croissant and butter, hardly the subject of an international coverup. But anyone who dared to call Mrs. Mulroney's office or the prime minister's office, for details on Mila's stolen afternoon with Nancy was curtly rebuffed. (My question was innocent. I merely asked: "What is this — Versailles?") No one would say — they still haven't said — how much the luncheon cost, who paid for it, who was invited. In official Ottawa, Mila is not only beyond the reach of access-to-information legislation, she is beyond criticism or doubt.

The Mulroney White House responds to all questions about the prime minister's wife in a tone of exasperated disdain: How dare you imply that Mila is anything less than perfect. Why are you picking on a *girl*? Getting an interview with her is as difficult as getting an interview with the Pope. Those few reporters granted audiences return with notebooks full of fluff, generic first lady stuff about how fortunate we are to be living in a democracy, how peace is generally preferable to war, etc. On tour Mila is often shadowed by expensively dressed charm-school graduates and deferential officials, who clear the corridors before she makes her well-timed entrance into a hall, then shield her from unfriendly questions on the way out. She has been known to give speeches that are frankly political, defending a Tory budget in western Canada, for example, or explaining Brian's deep concern for women's issues, then evading questions from reporters afterwards. Mila is a politician on the platform, but just a wife when she steps down. Once she was questioned about her right to office space on Parliament Hill, an ongoing controversy, while rushing to a charity event. She dropped her guard and replied in a complaining tone: "Why would you trouble me with this when we are going to this [I.O.D.E. fundraiser]?" Mila loves cameras but she hates questions.

In the absence of hard evidence, we can only conclude that the elegant luncheon that blustery April afternoon was Mila's personal gesture to her spiritual leader, her way of saying thanks to Nancy for coming to cold, small Ottawa in such a bleak month. The treasury won't collapse under the weight of one extravagant gesture, but the incident does tell us something about Mila's imperial, and occasionally imperious style. So did the events of the following week. In the worthiest piece of investigative journalism of the year, the *Globe and Mail* revealed that the Mulroneys borrowed more than 300,000 dollars in Tory party funds to renovate 24 Sussex. Tories were aghast as details of the financing emerged; ordinary Canadians were appalled and titillated to learn that some of the money was spent on closets large enough to house fifty pairs of prime ministerial Guccis. As for Mila, overnight Miss Goody Two-Shoes became Miss Goody Too-Many-Shoes.

It was Brian who faced the questions afterwards, but Mila who orchestrated the redecorating effort, indulging her taste for the finest fabrics and antiques, for wallpaper to which she demanded and got world rights. The comparison with Imelda was too tempting to ignore, and no one did. Who can erase the image of Mila ordering workers to replace a carpet three times because the colour wasn't right, or upholstering Nicolas' crib bumper-pad to match his room?

If Mila was just another Westmount housewife she would be perfectly entitled to her caviar lunches in Paris, the shopping sprees in Rome, the gold jewellry, raw-silk suits and exquisite clothes — the worldly style that provides opposition backbenchers with such a reliable supply of material. She would have every right to brush past the thrusting microphones and the impertinent questions. But Mila is a public figure, a national celebrity, even, if *Chatelaine* magazine is to be believed, a role model for Canadian women. She has turned her private life — the kids, her Serbo-Croatian parents, the Christ-mas-card togetherness — into a political commodity. She shouldn't be surprised that everything she does (and everything she buys) has political meaning.

Mila's problem is that she wants it both ways. She continues her inflationary spending habits, while her husband's government preaches restraint. She eagerly courts national celebrity, then bristles at questions about her political views or her private life. Mila was furious when the press speculated that she might be pregnant with Nicolas before she had a chance to tell her parents. Yet she apparently doesn't object when her husband uses the baby as a prop for the media. During the Reagan summit, Mulroney deliberately brought two-year-old Nicolas outside 24 Sussex to parade him before bored photographers, introducing the child as "my new min-ister of youth," while cameras whirred. The picture made all the papers the next day — as Mulroney knew it would.

There is another example of Mila's double standard. From the beginning she advertised herself as a stay-at-home wife and mother, part of a marketing strategy aimed directly at traditional Tory voters. Yet behind the scenes she is more intimately involved in her husband's career than any wife since Olive Diefenbaker. Given her devotion to hearth and home, it is ironic that she is the first prime minister's wife to conspicuously occupy a suite of offices in the PMO, furnished with antiques and loans from the Art Bank and staffed by three full-time assistants. Mila even represented Canada at Nancy

Reagan's 1985 First Ladies' Summit on Drugs as if she was a real diplomat — she brought along a briefing book and her own bureaucrat — an unprecedented presumption by a political wife. She will likely campaign independently during the next election campaign, following the example of her friend Nancy Reagan. "I'm a political animal," Mila once said, in a rare moment of candor. "I love it." More than any other political wife, Mila has turned her job into another branch of government.

This does not, alas, give feminists much joy. Mila has power all right, but it's that old-fashioned kind of female power, dishonestly acquired and fraudulently maintained. Brian once spoke admiringly of Mila's abilities:

> Her judgment, which is partly based on gut, partly on intuition, partly on reflex, is remarkable. Absolutely remarkable. For people, for issues, for political solutions. Just amazing. It's a good thing people don't know how influential she is.

What a revealing addendum! What it means is that Mila has to exercise her influence covertly, hide what she really thinks, and move silently behind the curtains to get what she wants.

The deception is indulged, even admired by her husband and his aides; they see nothing wrong with "feminine wiles," even though the notion is a sexist relic which applauds women for using seduction and fraud rather than frank effort to get what they want. Brian may think it is cute — it tells us something about what he thinks of women in general — but a lot of other people don't. As one political wife says tartly:

> If Mila wants to be a politician, she should run for office herself. She has no more right giving political speeches than a brain surgeon's wife has a right to wander into the operating theatre and take over her husband's job.

Feminism was all about women earning power, not marrying it.

It isn't only feminists who object to Mila's behind-the-scenes manipulation; it is anyone who cares for democratic nicety. After all, Mila was never elected to anything and represents no one. She doesn't even have the political legitimacy of a humble backbench MP. She has no right offering political advice, participating even obliquely in cabinet debates or pulling any levers. When she claimed credit for persuading the government to increase funding for medical research — a cause dear to her heart, because her father is a prominent Montreal doctor — there was bad-tempered and quite justified grumbling on Parliament Hill. What right has Mila to use the public treasury as her private charity? If her dad was a general would the armed forces finally get the nuclear-powered submarines they want so badly?

Such questions are repeated, *sotto voce*, by the cabinet ministers who occasionally receive businesslike memos from Mila's office calling their attention to some bureaucratic oversight and insisting on immediate reparation. Mila once said that she forwards letters she receives from immigrants to the multiculturalism minister (then Otto Jelinek) with a note saying something like: " 'This is a letter I have received, Otto, please look after it.' I then follow it back and say Otto, what did you do with that letter?"

Mila is impatient with excuses. She clearly sees herself as an ombudswoman for the little people, an Evita of the frozen pampas. As she explained to the *Toronto Star*:

> People are very candid with me. Maybe they have gone directly [to a cabinet minister] and they want to see what happens if they go to me. And you know, if it works, maybe they'll approach me again. And if it doesn't work, maybe they'll go back to the minister. It's another way, I suppose, of being a good support system.

It all sounds very mild, but Mrs. Mulroney's office has acquired a reputation in certain circles for being a tad high handed.

Mila is careful not to pick fights with feminists; she even quotes Betty Friedan approvingly. (The new Friedan, not the old. The new Friedan has moved from a lament for the limitations of the traditional role for women in the *Feminine Mystique*, to an impassioned defence of the nuclear family in *The Second Stage*.) Mila appropriates the language of feminism to defend her traditional style; she isn't pushing her wifestyle on anyone, she says, she is merely exercising her right to choose. She is pioneering the dubious concept of serial equality; once Brian is finished with politics, it will be *her* turn to have a career. She makes speeches calling on women to take leadership roles and she insists that her daughter, Caroline, is going to finish school — unlike Mila, who dropped out of engineering a few credits shy of a degree. However she also tells her daughter, "We must attain our goals without being aggressive. In our society there is room for everything, but aggression scares me." In other words, be a feminist, but remember you are a lady too.

Mila is not so much anti-feminist as post-feminist. You see them in *Chatelaine* and elsewhere, wearing wide leather belts and telling everyone that you can have it all — money, power, children and clothes. Post feminists are not explicitly anti-feminist; they have simply transcended the need for feminism. In their tidy world, feminism is, like adolescence, merely an awkward stage on the road to full maturity, unfashionably extreme and unattractively intense. Post-feminists are happy collaborators and tough bargainers, ready to serve as hand-maidens to a patriarchal political culture in return for special treatment — their own campaign jet, national celebrity, an unlimited expense account, political influence. They make a virtue of wealth and good grooming and downplay accomplishment or spiritual depth. They substitute charity for social justice. They sentimentalize motherhood, ignoring the fact that it is a costly option, increasingly available only to the nanny class. They don't earn power through their own efforts; they acquire influence through marriage and exercise it through manipulation. The subtle message to young women, transmitted by an often unquestioning media, is this: find an ambitious man and he will pull you to the summit. All you forfeit is your independence — a trivial price to pay for the vicarious delights of second-hand power.

Post-feminists claim that, unlike their pre-feminist sisters who were stifled by the lack of opportunities for their gender, they have *chosen* to be subservient. They willingly and consciously put themselves second, even third, to their husbands and children and advertise that choice as a bold exercise in personal freedom. It seems a dubious liberty, but Mila, for one, insists that she is not oppressed; she wants to be a wife and mother at this stage of her life. Nothing wrong with that. We all chose at various times to put someone or something else — children, husband, lover, job — ahead of our own personal wishes. That compromise is part of living in the world. But the role of political wife *institutionalizes* subservience for women; it casts wives in a secondary role in all aspects of life (except interior decorating) for as long as they remain political wives. This half-life, this life on parole, is not considered in the least infamous; it is eulogized by our male political culture as proper, normal, even noble.

It is also hard for feminists to attack. Mila is not oppressed, depressed or repressed in any obvious way. In fact career women recognize that they are in the presence of another professional, and not an unassuming housewife, when Mila is around. Isn't criticizing her choice to be a mother and wife a denial of choice? It would be, except that Mila is hardly a typical wife and mother, despite her protestations to the contrary. Unlike the prime minister's wife, few women marry men who can afford to support them, even if that is what they want. Fewer still have nannies. Most women with young children are poor, financially dependent on men or seriously sidelined in their careers. Mila touched a nerve when she said she was going to bring Nicolas into work after he was born. "I look forward to having a playpen in my office," she said.

> I think many working mothers do that, and I'm going to enjoy every bit of time I can spend with him. . . . I'd like to see it become an option for women to do that — I think it would be nice if women could continue having families and their work. I think employers are sufficiently open-minded today and they see that women are an asset in the workplace.

Noble sentiments, but not everyone works for an "open-minded" employer who also happens to be her husband. What do you do with a baby in a restaurant kitchen or a cow barn or a hospital ward? While Mila muses, her husband's government toys with a national child-care program that is insultingly inadequate. Whether she means to or not Mila promotes the fiction that motherhood is valued in our society, when it isn't valued at all. It's sentimentalized.

Part of the problem with wanting things both ways is that you get flack from all sides. In January 1987, when Mila, the full-time wife and mother, flew off to Europe and Africa with Brian hours after her middle son Ben, then ten years old, was injured in a schoolyard accident, there were disapproving frowns all across the country.

Even some PC parliamentary wives privately questioned Mila's judgment. Obviously aware of the dangers of a political backlash, Brian and Mila set out on a deliberate walkabout among the press contingent on the plane carrying them abroad that January day, stopping to explain to every reporter how badly they felt about Ben, how torn they were. As Mila told one correspondent, "I hated to leave him, but he was so good — he told me to go." She told another: "He's [Ben] not well. But he'll be all right. There is really nothing I can do you know. My mother is there. My mother-in-law is there."

Brian told reporters the accident put things into perspective. The boy's back injury — he fell from a swing — was serious, but not life threatening. He was bedridden for a couple of days. No one doubted that the Mulroneys' concern for their son was sincere, or that Mila is a devoted and responsible mother. It was the deliberate strategy of political containment on the airplane that day that looked inexcusably cynical.

Politics aside, Mila was probably perfectly justified in leaving her son behind; any working mother facing conflicting demands would certainly sympathize. Except that by 1987 it was hard to swallow the fiction that Mila is the typical working mom. It is hard to sympathize with someone who has apparently unlimited financial resources, a nanny, a job that basically involves smiling and shopping and presents no pressing reason for travelling half-way around the world especially when your son is recovering from an accident. Mulroney's staff tried to persuade reporters that Mila had "important official duties" on the Africa trip, but her only real function was to stand by Brian's side in photo ops, attend a few banquets and, an irony that did not escape the reporters accompanying her, make media visits to afflicted African children. Everyone knows being a political wife isn't a real job. Cynical reporters speculated that Mila just didn't want to miss a foreign shopping opportunity.

Former Liberal party president Iona Campagnolo once said being a political wife, "is the most thankless job in politics." It is certainly one of the most trying. Mila is criticized on one hand for being a traditional wife and mother, and on the other for being too politically involved. She is admired for her appearance, her clothes and her glamour, yet criticized for spending too much money on things. Some people want her at her husband's elbow every time he ventures out; others find her smiling presence ridiculous and unnecessary.

Apart from that, there is an admirable strength about Mila that even her coquettish deceptions and evasions can't disguise. Mila isn't an insubstantial person, some flighty airhead who bobs like a wooden duck on the waves of public opinion, nor is she a simple housewife who lacks the confidence to leave the kitchen. She is smart, ambitious and political. She is widely credited with holding the marriage together during some rocky years, of convincing Brian to quit drinking. Her strength may spring from her Serbo-Croatian roots, from her conservative unbringing, from a culture that honours hard work and rewards success. It may come from her profound belief in her notion of family.

Mila Pivnicki was born a Serbian and she still speaks the language with her four children. She and her younger brother came to Canada with their mother when Mila was five, to join their father, Dimitrije Pivnicki in Montreal. Her father, now a prominent psychiatrist, went to medical school here and, at first, the family lived in a modest Montreal apartment. Mila often refers to those difficult times, especially to counteract news stories about her extravagance, but the truth is that she came from a professional background; her Yugoslavian grandfather was a lawyer, not a peasant. In Montreal, Mila attended Miss Edgar's and Miss Cramp's private school, an exclusive institution for wealthy Westmounters, and grew up in a comfortable upper-middle class milieu. Like many ambitious immigrants, Mila became almost totally assimilated — more Westmount than the Westmounters — although she remains very close to her family, to her parents who live in Montreal, and to her Yugoslav roots. Her ethnicity may partly explain the contradictions in Mila's behavior, in her public persona. Like many immigrants, she has worked very hard to conform to North American values — attracted by the materialism, the achievement ethic, the competitiveness of this society. On the other hand, she is strongly drawn to a more conservative, old-world notion of wife and family.

Yet there is a cold arrogance about Mila that discourages sympathy. She doesn't have the grace to be embarrassed when her excesses are exposed; instead, she is just irritated. Asked about her profligate spending in a September 1986 interview (pre-Guccigate), the prime minister's wife replied wearily, "I've learned in public life you are criticized no matter what you do, so I'm just going to keep living my life as normally as possible." And bring me four more of those thousand-dollar vases, Giovanni.

There is also something breathtakingly cynical about the way she allows herself to be used by her husband's political machine. There is nothing wrong with loyalty to a spouse, but everything Mila says, wears and does is calculated to help her husband. It is as if she has subsumed her own personality entirely. Attractive, slender and fifteen years younger than Brian, she has become a living reflection of his taste and power. "That's for me," he reportedly said when he first saw nineteen-year-old Mila in a bathing suit beside a Montreal country-club pool. As if she was a commodity. To his political cronies she is a commodity, of course, a political commodity. Mila's "feminine" qualities — her glamour, her girlish giggling and her flirtatious way — are marketed aggressively, while her intelligence and political acuity is downplayed. Nor is she above batting her eyelashes to charm male voters or reporters. One male reporter who wrote something mildly critical about Mila during the '84 campaign remembers being singled out by her the next day for a public dose of flattery and friendly teasing. Mila didn't necessarily write this sexist script, but she has to take some responsibility for her own part. She behaves the way girls were supposed to behave in pre-feminist days: coy, strategically weak, artful. For a lot of people it is a tiresome and offensive routine. If only she would be herself — whoever that is.

Back at the National Arts Centre that windy April day, a solitary reporter and an amateur television film crew had the back door staked out, waiting for Mila and Nancy to emerge from their elegant luncheon. Along the drive- way sat eight shining limos, their engines idling. Large American security men with earphones loitered men- acingly. Then came the first sign that the secret party was breaking up: a large German shepherd emerged, dragging his Mountie handler along the red carpet that lead to the waiting limos. The television lights went on. Nancy blinked like a frightened animal when she saw them, then fixed a smile on her face. Mila twinkled like an eager star by her side. Then two protesters jumped up, two young women in flowered cotton dresses and Palestinian scarves, holding a tattered white banner: Stop Toxic Rain. An unwelcome intrusion of political reality into the serene afternoon of a political wife. Mila wrin- kled her nose, smiled a cold, cold smile at the protesters then rushed into the waiting limo and was gone.

FIVE

The miracle of hairspray

NANCY REAGAN SELLS AN AMERICAN VISION OF WIFELINESS AND, AS USUAL, CANADA IS THE BEST CUSTOMER

"To accent her interest in young people, the First Lady often appears in public with children at her side."

U.S. News and World Report, October 1984

AMERICANS EXPORT TRENDS THE way we export lumber. Ideas, notions, styles splash across our border every day and run in thin rivulets into every small community, every remote corner of the country. There are no non-tariff barriers when it comes to trends, not even good taste. So it isn't surprising that even in the esoteric domain of the political wife we've taken the lead from our American cousins. Historically and constitutionally there is no place for a "first lady" in Canadian public life, but because the Americans have a first lady we have to have a first lady — even if we can't call her that. What that means in the age of Reagan is that we have to have our own Nancy.

This is especially true in the late eighties, in the age of Mulroney. Brian and Mila's relationship to Ronnie and Nancy can be seen as a metaphor for the present relationship between Ottawa and Washington, at least the relationship Brian would like to establish. He is the dutiful son-in-law trying to impress his powerful relation with his industry and his goodwill, and Mila is Nancy's most promising apprentice, an admiring daughter learning how to keep her man happy and, more to the point, in power. Just as the relationship between Canada and the United States is made clear in the metaphor, so is the relationship between husband and wife. In both cases, one partner is much more important than the other.

The free trade talks are the political expression of the Mulroney approach, but Brian is a continentalist in far more than his politics. He is a continentalist in his bones.

Ever since he was a boy in Baie Comeau, singing "Dearie" for Colonel McCormick, the Chicago newspaper baron who built the northern Quebec pulp town, Brian revered rather than despised the foreign boss. Like many an ambitious lad from a company town, he was more interested in ingratiating himself with those remote, powerful forces than overthrowing them. Brian got fifty dollars for singing to McCormick, and he said when he gave it to his mother she almost had cardiac arrest.

In later life he moved to a larger stage, but the refrain was essentially the same. Working for the Iron Ore Company, commuting frequently between head office in Cleveland and Montreal, he seemed to regard the Canada-US border as an inconvenience more than anything else. Like any self-respecting multinational executive, Brian and his attractive corporate wife lived and thrived in what is essentially an American culture. His whole life was a rehearsal for the moment that he sang "When Irish Eyes are Smiling" with Ronnie at the Shamrock Summit in Quebec City in 1985.

This admiration for America has spilled over into imitation. There are small things, such as the way our cabinet ministers now insist on being called "Minister Carney" or "Minister Clark," a direct copy of the American "Secretary Shultz," and amusing things like the way Brian hauls a podium embossed with the seal of office everywhere he goes, just like Ronnie. Far more significant is the way the Mulroneys are marketing themselves as a Political Couple, a concept the Americans first test-marketed with John and Jackie Kennedy and perfected with Nancy and Ronnie. As journalist Robert Fulford wrote recently: "Mila Mulroney's elevation to First Lady — slow and careful though it has been — is part of the Americanization of Canada."

If Canada had a First Lady it would be Governor General Jeanne Sauvé, or the Queen, or even the wife of a male governor general. Except in newspaper headlines, the concept does not exist in Canadian tradition. But at the Shamrock Summit in Quebec City, Sauvé was figuratively shouldered aside so that Mila could mount the stage with her husband and assume the role of official hostess — whether we liked it or not. Many people didn't, and Mila has been much more discreet ever since. Jeanne Sauvé even raised a vice-regal fuss — she can manipulate the media with the best of them — and, since then, she has been on prominent display at all official functions. Not that Brian and Mila have abandoned their dream of being just like Ronnie and Nancy.

The Reagans have a slight advantage over the Mulroneys, of course, because both are actors by profession, not only by circumstance. Both are also working from a very successful script. Ronnie is the most popular president in years (if you discount his policies, which an astonishing number of Americans appear ready to do), and Nancy, after an uncertain start, has won the fond affection of her people at last. Together they have turned the presidency into a job for two people, a televised family drama. Nancy even appeared on the popular "Family Ties" TV program to promote her anti-drug campaign. The Americans have always been better at sitcoms than anyone else, certainly than Canadians.

As with all sitcoms, everyone's role is rigidly defined. Ronnie's job (keeping the world safe for capitalism) is more important, of course, but Nancy's has profound symbolic meaning. Laval University film professor Paul Warren described Nancy's performance at the 1985 Shamrock Summit at Quebec City in *Le Soleil*. He wrote: "Nancy Reagan only exists to prove there is a Ronald Reagan. More precisely, her function is to watch him." Ronnie once said admiringly of the woman he calls Mommie: "She [Nancy] is my echo chamber." As she stands, two steps back, her large eyes brimming with matronly concern, Nancy is a vehicle for some very old ideas about women, family and the American Way. "My first priority is my husband. Always," Nancy says, unapologetically. For Mila, "Brian comes first."

Mila is generally more discreet than her husband, her enthusiasms and her irritations more veiled. So it is hard to judge her true relationship with Nancy. Both women try to make the relationship look warm, although one senses in Nancy a certain regal distance. One senses in Mila an eagerness to impress. In August 1986, *Toronto Sun* columnist Claire Hoy reported that Mila commissioned three hundred handcrafted porcelain jewellry boxes shaped like 24 Sussex to hand out to special guests, similar to the White House replicas that Nancy distributes in Washington. Hoy also reported that Mila asked her Mountie guard to salute her because the US secret service salutes Nancy. The reports were heatedly denied

and a furious prime minister suggested that only someone "with a streak of cruelty" would write such a thing.
He told the Commons, humorously, that Mila, as an
immigrant, would probably salute the Mounties rather
than vice versa. (Behind the scenes, the story so infu-
riated the prime minister that he reportedly pressured
Hoy's employers to get him out of town. Hoy, a reliable
reporter, stands by his story.)

Then there was the gala benefit hockey game that Mila
organized with Edmonton millionaire Peter Pocklington
in September 1986 to raise money for her pet charity,
cystic fibrosis. That was pure imitation. A black-tie crowd
bought tickets for 5,000 dollars, watched a first-rate hockey
game in a drafty Ottawa arena, then headed over to the
National Arts Centre to be entertained by one of the
Reagan court entertainers, Dinah Shore. The gala was
very much in the American style — at least the style
favoured by Ronnie and Nancy's wealthy California
friends. It was a brash, posh, candlelit affair, complete
with fleets of black limos, an exclusive cocktail party
beforehand at 24 Sussex and a sumptuous dinner in
elegant surroundings after — the kind of event that
highlights the differences between recipient and
donor in a way more discreet fundraising methods or
government-funded programs don't. Everyone goes
home feeling better about being wealthy. As the *Kingston
Whig-Standard* sniffed:

> There is an element of tackiness about the event's public
> nature that offends. . . . Canadians who have respect-

able incomes traditionally do not enjoy flaunting their wealth in the way that many Americans do.

For Brian and Mila, who give the impression that they struggled hard all their lives so they could afford vacations in West Palm Beach, there is obviously nothing wrong with "flaunting" wealth. They seem, in keeping with Tory orthodoxy, to equate it with success. That explains not only the expensive redecorating effort at 24 Sussex (the 100-dollar-a-roll wallpaper and closet space for hundreds of shoes) but the unapologetic and unembarrassed reaction to the story by the prime minister and his wife. Mila has carried her imitation of Nancy so far that she is even copying the first lady's mistakes.

In the early days, Nancy's *ancien régime* style and the apparently endless supply of 5,000-dollar Galanos suits and dresses inspired full-colour spreads in leading US magazines on the return of elegance to the White House — and sharp reprimands. The consumption was too conspicuous for some. On Reagan's inauguration night, a public transit record was set when four fur coats were reported lost on Washington's subway. The four-day extravaganza to welcome the Reagans to Washington cost eight million dollars and ushered in a return of white-tie receptions and the wearing of service medals at official functions. *Newsweek* called it "a dubious evocation of the court of Versailles." Newspapers freed up specific reporters to cover The Wardrobe, and nothing else. Soon their beats had to be expanded to include wallpaper and china.

Before the Carters had even moved out of the White House, Nancy had L.A. interior designer Ted Graber, the so-called First Decorator, measuring for carpets. She spent 700,000 dollars renovating the living quarters in the White House and another 200,000 dollars on new china — an impressive sum compared to the paltry 310,000 dollars the Mulroneys spent sprucing up 24 Sussex six years later. It was donated money, but the extravagance didn't go over well in a country that was eliminating school lunches for ghetto kids. As journalist Jane O'Hara wrote in *Maclean's* magazine, Nancy's "let-them-eat-jelly-beans" attitude swiftly became a public relations disaster.

In 1981 *Newsweek* ran a poll which said that 68 percent of Americans thought Nancy was too concerned with style and fashion. (What a cruel irony, after a lifetime of dressing to please everyone but herself.) Sixty-one percent thought she was unsympathetic to the poor and underprivileged. Most appalling, she ranked fourth in popularity among the six most recent first ladies. Still first in American hearts was Jackie (no penny-pincher herself, ironically enough); second was Rosalynn Carter, the wife-secretary who attended working lunches with her husband once a week and acted almost as co-president; then Betty Ford, who set a new standard in frankness by talking about her breast surgery and her drug and alcohol problems; then Nancy. Trailing badly were Lady Bird Johnson and Pat Nixon, the woman with the hair-sprayed personality.

The poll caused immense consternation in the White House and an emergency team was assembled, made up of four of the president's personal advisers and key members of Nancy's staff. They held several meetings in 1981 and 1982 exclusively devoted to the remaking of the president's wife. First, they banished some of her questionable friends, especially wealthy New York bachelor Jerry Zipkin, described in *Time* as a "full-time Manhattan party-goer" and by Nancy as "a modern day Oscar Wilde." As a child Nancy travelled in a somewhat bohemian circle with her actress mother, and to this day her closest friends are in the film industry. But political wives do not have the luxury of liking just anyone. Their friends must be as suitable as their footwear. (Curiously, Frank Sinatra and "Dynasty" star Joan Collins escaped the purge, which proves that if you have enough money and fame in America, any amount of bad taste will be overlooked. But you do need a great deal of both.)

A self-described "chronic worrier," Nancy was also stiff and rather remote in public in her early days. The White House wizards decided she needed a sense of humour. They got one of the president's speechwriters, Landon Parvin, to insert some self-deprecating jokes into a speech Nancy gave at a New York fundraiser. The jokes were widely reported. Nancy gamely commented on a satirical postcard then in vogue, "Queen Nancy," which showed her wearing royal attire and a crown. "Now that's silly," Nancy wisecracked. "I would never wear a crown. It messes up your hair." She added that her latest project was "the Nancy Reagan home for wayward china." Brian Mulroney tried the same tact the week after the embarrassing revelations of Guccigate, at a Parliamentary Press Gallery dinner. He apologized for being late, explaining that, "Nicolas got lost in our shoe closet and it took us an hour to find him."

What Brian and the boys in Ottawa admire more than anything about the Reagans is the sheer professionalism with which the American couple manipulates public opinion. Got a public relations problem? Simple to fix. Get a new script. When hardcore Washington reporters started to snicker about The Gaze — the adoring look with which Nancy followed Ronnie's every word — she dropped it from her repertoire, or at least toned it down. "I'm trying not to do it as much as I have done it in the past," she explained to *Time* magazine in January 1985. "Only because there was so much talk about it, and it was kind of ridiculed." Nancy has a staff of twenty-four, her own press agent, her own "projects" director, her own chief of staff. She has a photographer assigned exclusively to her. Their task is to present the first lady in a favourable light. Every smile is calibrated, every handshake calculated. Nancy is an entirely prefabricated public figure.

When people began to whisper that Nancy had too much power, that she was running the White House, the president's image-makers went on red alert. How could the country respect itself in the morning if it found out a woman was in charge? During Ronnie's first term in office, the Reagans were forced to create a ludicrously transparent lie to cover up one unwelcome intervention by Nancy. At an informal press scrum in California Reagan hesitated when someone asked a question on arms control. Within earshot of reporters, Nancy whispered, "We're doing everything we can." Reagan dutifully repeated, "We're doing everything we can." Later the Reagans insisted Nancy had not been prompting him, but merely talking to herself. (Ronnie's hair is naturally black, too.)

Then, during the Irangate scandal, word leaked out that Nancy was gunning for former White House chief of staff Donald Regan. There were deliberately planted reports of an acrimonious telephone conversation, during which Nancy hung up on Regan. There were other reports that Ronnie told his beloved wife to "get off my goddam back," and stop pestering him about his staff problems. None of this came as a surprise to the people close to Reagan. They knew of Nancy's reputation as a ferocious hitman for her husband; Washington was said to be strewn with her victims.

As Robert Fulford wrote of Olive Diefenbaker, "a good political wife holds her husband's opinions, only more so." But by 1987, with only a few months left in her husband's term, Nancy dropped her habitual reserve and ventured an opinion of her own. With uncharacteristic asperity, she refuted charges that she was meddling, that it was a henpecked presidency:

> Although I don't get involved in policy, it's silly to suggest my opinion should not carry some weight with a man I've been married to for thirty-five years. I have opinions; he has opinions. We don't always agree. But neither marriage nor politics denies a spouse the right to hold an opinion or the right to express it.

Nancy must have sensed that she had nothing to lose, or realized she had already won. Donald Regan, of course, is history.

What Nancy needed even more than a personality overhaul, was a cause. Every first lady needs a cause. It justifies her life of idleness and privilege, and reflects well on her husband. He cares by proxy. Compassion by association. As a gracious lady living in California, before the Reagans moved to Washington, Nancy's main preoccupations were decorating their various residences and planning charity events with society friends like Betsy Bloomingdale — although it has been suggested that she was keener on redecorating than on charity. Nonetheless, while Ronnie was governor of California, Nancy did take on the Foster Grandparents program as a sort of starter charity. It had the great advantage of combining adorable children with loveable old people. In other words, photo opportunities to die for.

In the tough-minded Washington of the early eighties something more was needed. Old people and sick kids were too safe. Nancy had to capture public attention with a cause bold enough to erase her image as a callous socialite, and serious enough to establish her as a Woman of Content, a Person in her own Right among women voters. She had to answer feminist complaints about prominent wives acting as mere adjuncts to their husbands. She needed an independent identity, an obsession of her own. Some advisers thought a campaign against drug use among young people had just the right combination of pathos and passion. As *Time* magazine reported with unembarrassed candor, the "serious-minded display of the First Lady's social conscience" was shaped by two key aides, "as part of an overall effort to make her appear more caring, less frivolous." Nancy considered a bit hard-hearted? No problem. We'll *build in* a social conscience. Other advisers argued against the idea, convinced that drugs was too depressing a subject and addiction a real downer. They lobbied hard for a "can-do" project with a self-help theme, the sort of charity dear to the hearts of the Reaganite right. When they couldn't come up with one, the war on teen drug use was born.

It was the perfect cause, because it united the moral majority — those who believe drug abuse is a sin rather than a social problem — with the earnest liberals working to rid inner-city America of the corner pusher. More important, the crusade posed no serious inconvenience to major campaign contributors. Had Nancy decided to tackle the two most deadly drugs in America, tobacco and alcohol, she would have walked right into unnecessary political turmoil. Besides, they are the drugs of preference among Nancy and Ronnie's pals. Another advantage of the war on street drugs is that the enemy is so unsavory. Everyone hates drug pushers (the kind who wear black leather and travel everywhere in the company of menacing dogs, not the dapper executives of the American Pharmaceutical Association). As a bonus, the victims of drug abuse often turn out to be both photogenic and articulate. The poor and visible minorities are well represented, too, so Nancy couldn't be accused of elitism. It soon became apparent that many of these reformed druggies could be counted on to break down as they recounted their heart-breaking struggle with addiction for the rolling cameras.

Like evangelical services, the success of Nancy's early anti-drug forays was measured by the number of tears shed. The more humidity the better. Nancy had teams of advance men lining up cooperative former addicts willing to play out their tragedies for the television crews. She recalled one appearance for Hugh Sidey of *Time* magazine in October 1986: "Three hours I spent there, and the kids would be crying, and the parents would be crying and I would be crying." If there was something voyeuristic in the performance, it made great television — and a great showcase for Nancy's new-found compassion.

Her concern wasn't entirely manufactured, even if her public appearances were. Two close friends of the Reagans — Art Linkletter and former actor Ray Milland — lost children in drug-related incidents, and those tragedies apparently touched Nancy's heart. Not that her caring ever slopped over into permissiveness. In interviews she made it clear that she found drug abuse "morally wrong," more a problem of individual weakness than social despair. She was convinced that no amount of federal money would relieve the problem, despite the bleatings of hard-pressed social agencies. As she told Hugh Sidey:

> I don't think throwing money at the problem is going to solve it. It's going to be solved by people standing up

and taking a position that it's wrong and they won't put up with it. It's morally wrong.

Ronald Reagan gave force to that belief in his 1986 budget, when he reduced the amount of federal money going into drug programs. In fact, one of the key functions of the modern first lady is to express the state's compassion for the suffering, to act as a stand-in for a real program of social justice. It costs far less to fund a first lady (except for Imelda) than it does to right social wrongs.

The image remake was a success. By January 1982 a *New York Times*/CBS poll showed Nancy had eclipsed her husband in popular appeal. She scored an approval rating of 71 percent, compared to 62 percent for him. Her anti-drug program was so succesful, Ronnie even tried to climb on the bandwagon himself, imposing mandatory drug testing on some federal employees in 1986. A number of well-publicized cocaine deaths among prominent actors and athletes in the mid-eighties couldn't have been better timed. They added urgency to Nancy's cause. The media loved it. In a generally favourable cover story in 1985, *Time* magazine reported on Nancy Reagan's Growing Role. This was a woman who had found her niche and, for once, wasn't redecorating it. *Time* excused Nancy's continuing preoccupation with expensive clothes by pointing out that she now had a Larger Mission and a New Assurance. The ever-syco-phantic Hugh Sidey described Nancy as,

> . . . a red-dressed dot of flame that by some alchemy has ignited the nation against drugs. As First Lady she

could have eased up, turned away into antiques or gardening. "But you couldn't, you couldn't, you just couldn't," she says, with the fervor of a healer that no one ever imagined dwelled in that 100-pound frame so elegantly cloaked and coiffed.

Sidey concludes, somewhat improbably: "She is so delicate that she seems to bend with every breath."

Emboldened by the glowing reviews, Nancy took her crusade to the world, organizing a first ladies' conference on drug abuse in Washington. Mila Mulroney attended, of course, and confessed she had been high once at a rock concert in Montreal. Not that she had smoked, she hastened to tell reporters. It was a contact high, caused by all the marijuana fumes in the air. (Can't you hear Margaret Trudeau laughing?) Picking up intuitively on the spirit of the event, Mila later got misty eyed for the cameras just like Nancy. As *Maclean's* reported: "When a sixteen-year-old reformed drug addict from Cincinnati broke down in sobs, while appearing before the assembled first ladies, Mulroney, like Nancy Reagan, fought back tears." The conference provoked a few spiteful asides — particularly over the spectacle of the first lady of Jamaica, Mitsy Seaga, insisting there was no drug problem on her island — but overall the publicity was good. A personal triumph for Nancy Reagan, that everyone in the White House hoped would pay off in political support for her husband. That, after all, is the point.

These days Nancy never goes anywhere without staging some kind of media event on drugs. In April 1987, when she came to Ottawa with Ronnie, she and Mila visited a local high school that was allegedly chosen for its drug program, although few of the students milling around among the security forces in front of the school before the presidential motorcade arrived seemed to have heard much about it. Inside, twenty handpicked students, social workers and community health experts sat in a circle in the school library, almost overwhelmed by a jousting circle of television and news photographers. Nancy and Mila sat in the circle, too, in an attitude of respectful attention, as their hosts ran through a carefully rehearsed series of questions and answers. Asked what she would do if offered drugs, Nancy replied, "I'd just say no." That's the slogan for her drug drive, and it is about as profound as her message gets. But for a first lady, the key thing is to create an *impression* of caring, not to do anything about drug abuse. And in the age of advertising, creating an impression just takes seconds.

Later in the school auditorium, the two women watched a Shakespearean farce that was studded with homophobic and sexist jokes, but apparently preferable to some harmless skits the students had written themselves for the Reagan visit. One of the original skits contained jokes about acid rain and Iran, and the prospect of real political content marring a first ladies' event frightened everyone senseless. Official censors from the prime minister's office and the White House suggested the offending skits be junked, and they were.

Indeed, throughout the Reagan visit the prime minister's office acted like an anxious colonial administration determined that nothing go wrong for the important visitors from the mother country. (It was as if Colonel McCormick himself was visiting.) The Mulroneys were so anxious to please they even imported an American social problem, drug abuse, so that they could apply the Reaganite cure — well-meaning rhetoric and shadowy funding. Never mind that the drug problem in Canadian schools in no way resembles the misery and despair of the drug culture in inner-city America. Brian is so anxious to imitate Ronnie that if the American president has a drug problem, Canada has to have an "epidemic."

As the media event at Brookfield High School wound down, Mila thanked Nancy in front of the students "for teaching me so much." One, or perhaps both of them, remarked that "youth is our future" and, following their detailed media itinerary to the minute, they were off with their hundreds of security men and advisers in their eight-car cavalcade at great speed. It was a surreal half-hour by any normal measure, a half-hour in which an Ottawa school and its students were used as a living backdrop for a larger morality play. It wasn't even a good play. Yet that is what first ladies do for their living. They star in brief and banal commercials for whatever social or political cause will help their husbands. Nancy is considered daring for embracing a controversial subject like drugs, so that the fact that she doesn't say or do anything but make safe and obvious remarks to television cameras is somehow overlooked. Mila, who probably has better instincts than Nancy, has so far avoided anything bordering on social relevance. But then she always plays it safe.

Is there a lesson in all this for Mila? Does Nancy have anything to "teach" her? Yes and no. To begin with, Mila doesn't have all the public relations problems Nancy had, despite Guccigate. She has never been publicly castigated for meddling in government business, for example, although some cabinet ministers watch her activities with nervous foreboding. There is growing criticism of her materialism and her extravagance, and she may soon be compelled to embrace some cause riskier than cystic fibrosis to prove that she cares about more than her next photo op or shopping trip. Undoubtedly, the image doctors in Ottawa will be studying Nancy's drug campaign as a sort of prototype.

It is quite possible that Mila will follow Nancy's example during the next election campaign, too, and do some touring on her own. She has said on a number of occasions that she is eager to campaign, that she loves it. She has made tentative campaign-style swings in the past. In 1986 she visited seventeen western cities and delivered twelve speeches defending her husband's economic policies. Actually, the speeches sounded more like paid party advertisements. She told one audience that Canada, "is starting to move again because of the Conservative party. It is a party of direction, new direction. And it is a party of change." She told reporters in Halifax that, "fiscal responsibility is wonderful when you're selling it, but when you're doing it it's not very glamorous." Mila was referring, of course, to government spending, not her own.

If she is judged an electoral asset in 1988 or 1989 (the polls will be all important), Mila may be pressed into service again. But her campaign will likely be more modest than Nancy's, partly because of cost and partly out of political sensitivity. During the 1984 American presidential campaign, Nancy toured in her own Air Force DC-9, a plane that seats forty-two, with three staffers, a White House photographer, an advance man, a nurse, four secret service agents and several reporters. For a time she shadowed Geraldine Ferraro, the first woman ever to run for vice-president of the United States. Nancy's covert mission was to undermine Ferraro, the Democratic candidate, by proving how much power and influence a traditional woman could have. See ladies, went the subliminal message, it is not only unfeminine, it is unnecessary to run for office yourself. Mila's approach may differ, but she is delivering essentially the same message.

Nancy Reagan is one of the miracles of hairspray. Hairspray is the glue that holds her image together, that keeps her ageless and timeless. The years of spraying have taken their toll. Her head has a cement-like cast; it looks too large and too heavy for the emaciated body. As well, you can see in Nancy's body language and demeanor, in her large open eyes, a kind of terror. To counteract it she has developed an almost superhuman inner control to match the outer mask. Garry Wills wrote of her in his book, *Reagan's America, Innocents at Home*:

> She [Nancy] practices a severe economy of expression that makes three or four compositions of the features cover all necessary social tasks — the smile of delighted surprise at the top of airplane stairs, the concerned gaze at redeemable druggies, and — most of all — the upward stare at her husband. In photograph after photograph one finds the same expression, not varied by a centimeter. It takes unsleeping vigilance to remain a somnambule, a political chastity symbol.

Unsleeping vigilance.

Reading between the lines of her autobiography (recited into a tape recorder in accord with current California literary style) there are glimpses of a woman whose other predominant emotion, next to fear, is gratitude. The gratitude may be a product of her personal history; she and her divorced mother were rescued from poverty when Nancy was seven by a prominent Chicago surgeon who married Nancy's mother and gave the little girl social standing and money in one swoop. It is as if, ever since, she has been trying to repay the debt, first to her adoptive father, then to the movie actor who replaced him. Nancy looks as if she doesn't think she really *deserves* her position and her privilege, even now in the final days of her reign. Her tense, gaunt body reveals her constant apprehension — fear of assassination attempts, fear of sin, fear of the terrible weakness of others, fear of anyone or anything different. No wonder she hangs on, with such desperate concentration, to the ground she has gained.

Mila isn't above stealing a few operational tips from the older woman, but she has something Nancy will never have: an inner confidence that sometimes looks like arrogance. Unlike Nancy, Mila appears to be untroubled by doubts about herself or her worthiness to play the role history has thrust upon her. She is every bit as controlled as Nancy Reagan, but her control springs from ambition, not fear. She will definitely outlast Nancy, and she may well eclipse her. In fact it is hard not to think of the president's wife in the past tense. As her husband approaches retirement, the air seems to be leaking out of Nancy Reagan. That must be what happens when you depend entirely on someone else's power and accomplishment to sustain you, to give your life purpose. When Ronnie leaves office, Nancy will turn to dry powder and blow away. Is there a warning there for the young, vibrant Mila?

Madame Jeanne St. Laurent and Louis in 1908, the year they were married.

Louis and Jeanne St. Laurent at the national Liberal convention in Ottawa in 1948.

Olive Diefenbaker presides over a reception for the Eisenhowers at 24 Sussex Drive in 1958.

Olive and John Diefenbaker with JFK and Jackie at 24 Sussex in 1961.

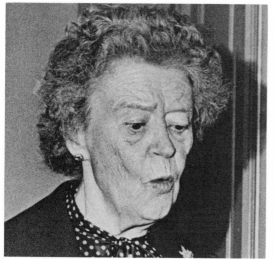

Maryon Pearson in 1978, shortly before her death.

[Ottawa Citizen photo]

Lester and Maryon Pearson shortly before their wedding in Winnipeg in 1924.

[Public Archives photo]

Margaret Trudeau in 1981.

Margaret Trudeau walks through downtown Ottawa in 1981.

Maggie and Pierre visit China in 1973.

A pregnant Maureen McTeer chats with an expansive Margaret Trudeau at an Ottawa party in 1976.

Maureen McTeer and Catherine ride in Rockcliffe Park in 1977.

Joe and Maureen on the campaign trail in June, 1983.

Alan Fotheringham and Mila Mulroney exchange squints at an Ottawa party in 1983.

Nancy Reagan and Mila Mulroney attend a drug seminar at an Ottawa high school in April, 1987.

Nancy and Ronnie say goodbye to Brian and Mila at Ottawa airport in April, 1987.

Nancy Reagan in her mink, with Ronnie and Governor-General Jeanne Sauvé during the Canada-US summit in April, 1987.

John and Geills Turner during the November, 1986, Liberal convention in Ottawa.

Lucille Broadbent in a domestic pose in 1984.

SIX

Amazing grace

MRS. OLIVE DIEFENBAKER AND THE
ERA OF THE POWER TEA

"The minute he became PM, I never opened my peeper again."

OLIVE DIEFENBAKER, 1965

FIRST OF ALL, NOBODY IS AS perfect as Olive Diefenbaker was supposed to have been. Nobody, with the possible exception of the Queen Mother, is as perpetually, invariably and consistently gracious. Nobody, apart from Mother Theresa, could spend twenty-three years married to the most obnoxious man in Canadian public life without once losing her temper. Nobody owned that many squat, cardboard hats with scraps of net hanging untidily from the front. Yet despite these self-evident truths, the cult of Olive persists almost thirty years after her reign.

To trash her memory now may seem churlish, jejune, mean-spirited. To attack her on feminist principles looks, if not absurd, at least overwrought. After all, Olive is dead; a black-and-white memory for most of us, a faint whiff of lavender. But her legacy lives on. In powerful circles in Ottawa she is still considered to be Canada's first and best political wife, a model for modern-day successors. What no one ever says is that it is a pernicious model, one that requires of women tremendous guile and self-abasement. It even threatens the return into common usage of the silver tea service.

Never mind. After the discontents of feminism, the memory of Olive is a beguiling vision for a certain kind of male politician: an adoring wife who never contradicts, never interferes and responds quickly to simple voice and hand commands. Olive knew her place and was content with it, unlike some of the young, restless political wives of today. There is a whole generation of women (my mother's) who never considered it an affront to wait on their husbands (or their children) and Olive was part of that generation. To all appearances, she was delighted to pour the tea and pass the cookies, while men handled the real business of the nation. More than that, she brought flair and elegance to this exalted form of waitressing.

In many ways, Mila Mulroney is Olive's natural successor. Although the two women come from different generations and backgrounds, they share a single-minded readiness to serve their husbands' ambitions above all else. Both have shown themselves capable of breathtaking control in a variety of settings; both appear to have a rod of steel running up their spines. Yet each has projected a deliberately "feminine" image: Olive the warmhearted matron and Mila the attractive, young corporate wife. Both had (have) strong marriages. Although they each have professed to be uninvolved in daily politics, both have acted as influential backroom advisers to their husbands. Indeed, it is easy to imagine that Mila and Olive could be more politically astute than Brian or Dief in certain situations. Each had the intelligence, flair and energy to succeed in politics on her own, but both chose to exercise power covertly. They even share the same flaw — a bright artificiality that raises doubts in the public mind about their sincerity and their depth. For Mila, the doubts have been building since she and Brian came to power in 1984. However, the true nature of Olive Diefenbaker didn't come to light until years after her death.

The *Toronto Star* was only repeating conventional wisdom when it wrote after Olive's death in 1976: "Of the various first ladies Canada has had since 1867, few have been as widely respected and admired as Mrs. Olive Diefenbaker." Olive was a Gracious Lady in the high-fifties, the Era of the Gracious Lady. It was also the heyday of the happy housewife, and Olive was an unofficial patron saint and an inspiration. Her life may have been a dizzying round of tea parties, bazaars and bouquet presentations, but her linens were always whiter than white. I remember seeing her on an escalator in Murphy-Gamble's department store in Ottawa once when I was a young girl. She ascended serenely, like a member of the Royal Family or a ship's figurehead, standing almost motionless on the moving stairway, smiling benignly on the shoppers scurrying beneath her. I was reminded of religious paintings depicting the Feast of the Assumption. Olive charmed politicians, tamed the media and won the protective affection of the entire country in a way that few public figures do. The fact that she is still idealized today is proof of the power of her appeal. It also proves how resistant our political elite is to innovation when it comes to the role of the political wife.

It wasn't until years later that people began to suspect that Olive was a bit of a fraud. Though she was admired by her contemporaries for her warmth, her smile and her hats, Olive's real strength lay in her political cunning, her tough-mindedness, her charisma and her formidable ambition. Indeed these qualities, the very ones that would have made her an excellent politician, were the ones she was forced to keep hidden. Why? Because they were male virtues. In her day, before feminism stalked the land, official Ottawa was unrelievedly male and had fixed notions about such things. Politics was a tough, dirty business that "normal" women sensibly shunned. Any display of cleverness, cynicism or wit was considered unseemly, as Maryon Pearson and other wives cursed with memorable personalities soon discovered. As for the accepted female virtues, beauty topped the list, followed by charm, tact, piety, discretion and, for political wives especially, a mindless, vacant pleasantness.

What was an intelligent woman with an interest in politics to do? What Olive did (and what Mila appears to be doing) was to redirect her own ambitions into her husband's career. There were intimidating barriers to women who wanted to run for political office themselves in the fifties and sixties, as there are today. Few had the family support or the cash. Who could blame an aspiring female politician for marrying a career, rather than trying to forge one on her own in such an unwelcoming arena? She couldn't get elected prime minister herself, so Olive pioneered the concept of the Political Couple in Canada. Brian and Mila are the most recent local manifestation, but it is a venerable tradition in the United States, and includes such successful teams as F.D.R. and Eleanor Roosevelt, John and Jackie Kennedy and Ronnie and Nancy, the most successful pairs act since world-champion figure skaters Barbara Underhill and Paul Martini.

It works simply enough; the husband becomes a sort of Trojan horse, who smuggles his wife into power along with him under cover of darkness. Publicly, the wife serves a purely decorative function (she hangs from his hand on public platforms, smiles and accepts bouquets) but behind the scenes she operates as a junior partner in the family firm. She delegates the housework and the "social" work to underlings (maids and nannies) and discreetly sets up shop in her husband's office. She becomes an unpaid, unofficial senior adviser on a whole range of policies and personalities. She develops her own public following and, often, her popularity eclipses her husband's.

This is no problem as long as she is admired for her warmth, her looks and her good works, and not for her ideas, her values or her political judgments. During the Irangate scandal in Washington, when strategic leaks suggested that Nancy Reagan had a contract out on the former White House chief of staff Donald Regan, there was a massive public backlash. Nancy was thought to be meddling, to be over-reaching, to be trespassing on the gritty male world of politics. Reagan's handlers worried that Nancy's ferocious strength would make their man look weak. How would Ronnie survive the disgrace of being beaten up by a girl? It is a problem Joe Clark and Maureen McTeer encountered, too: the sexist notion that if a wife is smart, tough and assertive that means her husband must be a wimp. It isn't a trap Olive or Mila ever fell into. They knew enough to keep their intelligence, ambition and political insights hidden.

In fact, to succeed as the female member of the Political Couple requires remarkable stealth. Olive always denied having any personal political aspirations, even when she was half of one of the most potent political partnerships ever seen in Canada. The ambitious political wife, however brilliant, pretends she is only along for the ride. She must never be seen to be directing or influencing her husband. When the conversation turns to policy, she keeps her "peeper" shut — at least in front of witnesses. Modesty prevents her from claiming any credit for her husband's successes, yet convention demands that she stand by him in his humiliations. If her husband blunders or breaks the law, she lies, fakes, feints and covers up for him no matter how culpable or how stupid he might have been. Pat Nixon is the apotheosis of this approach.

There is more than mere sexism at work here; there is democratic principle. Political spouses, male or female, have no political legitimacy because they are not elected. They have no right sitting at a cabinet table or even reading cabinet documents. They have no business trying to influence policy or lobby for special causes. Their only valid public functions were, and continue to be, largely symbolic, non-intellectual and secondary — in other words, functions ideally suited to women. *That* is where the sexism comes in.

Because she was neither docile nor stupid by nature, Olive had to be particularly devious. "The whole direction of my life is that I am John's wife," she frequently said, in a not entirely convincing display of feminine modesty. In truth Olive was a pro, a remarkably accomplished woman who made a name for herself in the larger world during a time when most women her age were housebound. Unlike Margaret Trudeau, Maureen McTeer and Mila Mulroney, she wasn't a young woman when she married into politics. She was in her mid-fifties, an experienced schoolteacher and a pioneer in the new field of educational guidance. She had spent seventeen years as a single mother, bringing up her daughter alone when her first husband died after three years of marriage. During a time when women were exceedingly scarce in the senior levels of bureaucracy, Olive was assistant director of guidance for the Ontario Department of Education, a job that, among other things, required her to travel around North America giving lectures. In 1953 she was about to be promoted to director when she quit to marry Dief, an old acquaintance who re-entered her life after years of separation. She took on wifedom as if it was another career. Unlike Margaret Trudeau, for instance, or even Maureen McTeer, Olive knew what she was getting into when she married.

From her wedding day on, everything Olive did was calculated to advance John's career. She assiduously courted the press, and the boys on the Hill (they were almost all boys in those days) were charmed. A lot of reporters no doubt envied Dief. Who wouldn't want an intelligent, accomplished wife acting as unpaid executive assistant and press agent? Besides stimulating their vestigial gallantry, Olive appealed to their news sense. She was a novelty after decades of bachelor prime ministers like Mackenzie King and R.B. Bennett, or stay-at-home wives like Jeanne St. Laurent. Like an exotic houseplant, Olive added colour and variety to the monotonous grey flannel of official life.

She also added a "human touch" to the political scene, a role that frequently falls to women. Men, and particularly prime ministers, are meant to be hard-headed, not soft-hearted. Compassion is the province of the wife, and Olive fulfilled her responsibilities in this area with unflagging dedication. In 1959 all the newspapers carried a story about the Diefenbakers' trip to London, during which a female chauffeur escorting the visiting couple around town accidentally scraped another car. Olive, sensing how upset the young woman was, unpinned a broach from her own coat and gave it to the chagrined chauffeur. Mysteriously, this impulsive, private gesture became national news. In his 1963 book, *Renegade in Power*, Peter C. Newman writes: "It was a measure of [Olive's] accomplishment, that she managed to transform her informal place in the official heirarchy into a position of considerable prestige." In modern terms, she gave the job profile.

More than that, Olive played a singular role in identifying and tagging the Canadian Political Wife as a separate species. When the Diefenbakers arrived in Ottawa, the city had been wifeless for decades. As wife of the leader of the Opposition, Olive began holding teas for wives of members of Parliament, to ease their way into official life, thereby granting official benediction and recognition to a hitherto untouchable caste — and earning

her husband new friends. She inaugurated the era of
the Power Tea in Ottawa, inviting people who might be
politically useful to Sussex Drive for (non-alcoholic)
afternoon refreshments. In their first three months in
power, Olive and John entertained some eight hundred
people. She poured tea and passed cookies, and soon
became recognized in political circles as that most valued
of commodities: a vote-getter.

Perhaps this explains the compulsive socializing, the
demanding schedule, the unceasing activity that seems
to characterize the lives of wives like Olive and Nancy
Reagan. They don't hold independent jobs, their children are gone and their domestic skills not really required.
Therefore they derive all their self-worth from helping
their husbands' careers. The more people they can charm
and win over, the more valuable their contribution and
the greater their own feeling of self-worth. For wives
who lack social skills, who are uncertain of the value of
all that frantic flattery, who are repelled by the notion
of stroking egos, life can be bleak indeed. Edna Diefenbaker, John's first wife, ended up in an asylum at least
partly because she couldn't cope with the social demands of her job. (In 1947, she wrote to John from their
Prince Albert, Saskatchewan home: "I have such an in-
feriority complex over myself, and with everyone down
there [in Ottawa] looking their best, I just can't face it.")
Perhaps the Power Tea and the obsessive activity it involves is an antidote to madness.

Not long ago at a dinner party, I asked a man who
had worked with Diefenbaker for years and knew Olive

well, what she was like. "In one word?" he replied. "Ruthless." In recent years there have been other hints that Olive's gracious manner disguised both an unlady-like taste for revenge and an inelegant mean streak. In his book, *Both My Houses*, published in 1986, a former Diefenbaker aide, Sean O'Sullivan, provides a vivid description of Olive as a sometimes spiteful woman who encouraged Dief in his worst excesses. "In public she ranks among the best political wives I've ever seen," writes O'Sullivan, who is now a Roman Catholic priest. "She could be smooth as a kitten's wrist. In private, however, her claws came out and she could be devastating. She carried enough bitterness and anger within her for both."

O'Sullivan, who became a Tory member of Parliament at the age of twenty largely because of a boyhood infatuation with Dief, also furnishes an anecdote to show how Olive's charm could mask her real intent. According to O'Sullivan, Olive was sitting in the House of Commons gallery beside another Tory member's wife, waiting for Dief to speak. The other member was recognized by the Speaker first and Olive was irked. As the anonymous MP started to speak, Olive turned to his wife and asked sweetly: "Is your husband not well?"

O'Sullivan also suggests that both Diefenbakers over-dramatized Olive's recurring illnesses. He recalls Dief coming into the office one morning and stating baldly: "Olive died six times last night." Another time, Olive told the young executive assistant: "You know Sean, I really shouldn't be going. I had a slight heart attack last night."

O'Sullivan's unsparing view of Olive is supported in another excellent book, *The Other Mrs. Diefenbaker*, a biography of Diefenbaker's first wife, Edna, by Vancouver journalist and former MP Simma Holt. Holt quotes Senator Josie Quart, a friend of both Diefenbakers, saying of the couple: "She [Olive] nurtured his paranoia." Holt's book, published in 1982, also suggests that while Dief's first wife, Edna, tried to talk Diefenbaker out of his irrational hatreds, Olive egged him on. Some critics have even blamed Olive for Dief's refusal to relinquish the party leadership gracefully in 1966, thereby setting the stage for Dalton Camp's successful regicide.

There is no doubt Olive had enormous influence with her husband, despite her *pro forma* disclaimers. ("My job as John's wife is to fit in as each duty comes up. It's not a political part. He's so ahead there, I could never catch up. I'm happy to adapt to the situation," she once said.) In reality, she was his closest confidante and there are indications in his memoirs and letters that he paid attention to her advice. In fact he phoned her frequently during a typical working day to read her an interesting letter, pass on a tidbit of the political gossip they both loved, or seek her reassurance about a speech. An excerpt from his memoirs concerning his first cabinet reveals how influential she could be:

> When I told Olive the names of those I had chosen, she, without attempting to interfere in any way, said "You

haven't included Jim Macdonnell." I said I could not.
She suggested it would break his heart. I reconsidered,
and, because of his war record and his many years of
work for the party, I decided to make him a minister
without portfolio.

Even in her love letters, she included hints for future
speeches, suggesting, in one note written in 1952 when
the two were courting, that John make a speech modelled
on "Pericles funeral oration over the Albemores who
died during the Peloponnesian Wars."

With no children to take care of (her daughter by her
first marriage was an adult) and no outside interests,
Olive was free to devote all her time to politics and did,
often sitting in the visitors' gallery to watch her husband
perform in Parliament. She was an energetic cam-
paigner, too, and crossed the country several times during five federal election campaigns, despite her continuing
back problems and arthritis. When he was giving a
speech, she often sent scribbled suggestions to the
podium, little asides designed to help him connect with
a crowd. Once in Cape Breton, she prompted: "We have
a painting of Cape Breton over our couch at home."

In his memoirs, Diefenbaker recalls another election
meeting in Chelmsford, Ontario, that got out of hand
when people outside the meeting hall started shouting
and shoving. Someone suggested Dief escape by the
back door, but he refused. So did Olive. As they made
their way through the mob, Olive reportedly jabbed one
protester with her elbow, causing him to double up in
pain, and Dief to double over in laughter. He later wrote:

> She stayed, as always, by my side. She was suberb. How much I now regret her being subjected to the brutal itineraries of five national election campaigns, during two of which she was on crutches. She insisted on being by my side. I could not have talked her into staying home.

Some of her hardships were, indeed, formidable. As the *Toronto Star* reported, with a touch of awe, in 1965: "She has learned to go for three weeks without getting her hair done professionally."

Being a fifties wife, Olive had routine duties as well. This was the period before Man learned to pack a suitcase, iron a shirt or match socks. Olive had to prepare John's clothes every time the couple travelled and serve as his informal dresser. An undated note from Olive included in Dief's letters, reads: "Wear white shirt marked X with new suit for opening — and new black and white tie. You will look really sharp!!"

As a woman she was also responsible for providing a homey nest. Dief's letters to his brother Elmer, many of them reproduced in the 1985 book, *Personal Letters of a Public Man*, are enlivened with frequent references to Olive's home redecorating efforts. In 1963 he wrote: "Olive bought a chesterfield yesterday and this evening she intends to go to a sale of antiques." Then later: "Olive is in Toronto today getting drapes etc. for the House. She has made it most liveable and attractive."

Interior decorating has always been a major part of a political wife's duties, but in the pioneering days women did much of the actual work themselves. When John and Olive were preparing to move into Harrington Lake — the prime minister's official summer home in the Gatineau Hills outside Ottawa — Olive made the curtains and slipcovers herself. How times have changed! Nowadays prime ministers' wives hire decorators before they even call the movers. In a fairly transparent imitation of the American style, every wife, even the serious-minded Maureen McTeer, has her own professional designer. Maureen used Ottawa architect Cecilia Humphrey and, until he disappeared to Italy leaving behind a number of unpaid creditors, Mila's man was interior designer Giovanni Mowinkel. It is said Mila used to call him in for consultation before she so much as bought a chair. By comparison, Olive was probably shopping for curtain fabric that day I saw her in Murphy-Gamble's.

In the end, Olive's most remarkable achievement may have been staying married to John Diefenbaker for twenty-three years. In private he could be even more egocentric, small-minded and difficult than he was in public. Forget those soft-focus images of the Old Chief in his dotage, a cranky but loveable Uncle Chichimus with a store of rambling anecdotes and a wicked, partisan wit. The man was mean. He was also vindictive, paranoid and hilariously petty as historical documents suggest and contemporary memoirs confirm. Eventually, even his own Progressive Conservative party discovered that a spellbinding after-dinner speaker does not always make the best prime minister (a lesson the Tories may be learning again) and stripped him of the leadership. Dief spent his final years sniping at his successors and planning a state funeral more elaborate than anything envisioned for even the Royal Family. He fretted endlessly over the list of honorary pallbearers, scratching names and adding others as people fell in and out of favour.

As a husband, John could be astonishingly selfish. When Olive came home from hospital in 1976, literally on the edge of death, he phoned her every fifteen to thirty minutes, as he always had, to read her letters, ask her advice, solicit her praise. Finally she had to ask one of his colleagues, MP Robert Coates, to intervene. "John keeps phoning me," Olive told Coates. "I am not well enough to handle it. Could you do something to stop him?" Even after death he would not leave her in peace. To the horror of her daughter, Dief had Olive disinterred from the cemetery in Ottawa three years after she died and flown to Saskatoon to be buried with him in the John Diefenbaker Centre.

One of the deeper mysteries of Canadian politics is how Olive stopped herself from murdering her beloved husband. There can be little doubt that his impossible personality, along with an impossible job, contributed to his first wife Edna's nervous breakdown. In September 1945, Diefenbaker had Edna admitted to a private sanatorium in Guelph for a series of shock treatments. Her psychiatrist Dr. Goldwin Howland wrote to Dief:

> She is a very fine woman, indeed, and her ideals are the best and she is completely wrapped up in your interests, but it would be better if she had more interests of her

own. She dislikes housekeeping, which is, unfortunately, part of her life's work.

He suggested John take her on a holiday when she got out of the sanatorium. "I do not feel certain whether starting her directly at work at home, is quite the wisest thing after such a serious illness." The patronizing tone was typical of the era and of mainstream psychiatry; it sounds as if the doctor is talking about a horse. It was obvious Edna needed something more than a vacation.

It can be misleading to measure human behavior against an ideological grid, especially at this distance, but it seems clear being a political wife helped drive Edna to an early grave — and put her in an asylum. Like Margaret Trudeau, she was suffocated by the strict rules that governed and still govern proper wifely behavior. These rules were hard enough on anonymous wives in Edna's day; for wives in the public eye, they were even more strict. Edna loved dancing, for instance, but had to give it up because her husband wouldn't participate and it was improper for a woman to go dancing with other men. (Olive, who liked classical music, painting, poetry and art, abandoned her pleasures too, because John didn't share them. She explained, "My recreations are John's, and none of those things are his.") Edna apparently wanted children but John didn't — at least not until Edna was forty-six and past childbearing. Nor was she encouraged to work. During the Depression, Edna had suggested going back to teaching, to help family finances. Replied John: "No wife of mine will ever work. And mother agrees with that." As Holt writes in her book: "She [Edna] had to narrow her life to suit his." Edna's friends apparently recall her saying, "John has three loves: his mother, politics and me — in that order."

If Olive was a fifties success story, Edna was an illustration of the cost of all that self-sacrifice. In one wrenching letter she wrote her husband while she was in the sanatorium, she scribbled in her hasty script:

> There must be someone who can tell why this stony [sic] feeling is here. . . . My brain is clear. It's just something has gone wrong with my nervous system. It's either drugs or the breakdown.

She pleaded with him to rescue her. "Please tell me you will come soon, otherwise I'll go clean crazy and disgrace you Dear, and so far I've been normal through it all." Edna, once a vibrant and popular fixture in official Ottawa, died of leukemia in 1951, at fifty-one years old, after twenty-two years of marriage. According to Holt's fascinating book, her confidence was shattered and her self-esteem in ruins. Who or what was crazy, Edna or the life she was expected to lead?

Two years later Dief remarried. While he was courting Olive in 1952, he displayed the sentimental side of his complex personality. "My Darling Ollie," he wrote in 1952. "Ollie, you're a darling — you couldn't have been sweeter than you were yesterday — and last evening as we parted — the smile of the angelic after the momentary tears." John Diefenbaker could be affectionate, particularly towards women, on whom he depended for love, support, companionship and political advice. Holt writes:

> From the earliest years of their marriage, she [Olive] learned of his dependency and knew that he was help-less without a woman close to him, not only to care for his basic needs in food, scheduling, packing, purchasing wardrobe for his frenetic career, but to monitor his words and activities, to advise and support him.

For some people, being needed that desperately is gratifying, as it apparently was to Olive. Against all the odds and despite their bitterness towards everyone else, Olive and John were happy together.

Olive not only survived as a political wife, she thrived. Although she suffered from painful illness throughout her public life, she was the envy of her contemporaries. She had it all: a good marriage, a gold-plated public image and a succession of large, friendly dogs who became national celebrities. (They were all called Happy.) Olive's strength seemed to come from the fact that she was so focussed on one thing — her husband's political wellbeing. There is a simplicity in that kind of obsession: all moral ambiguity and inner confusion are overcome by devotion to a transcendent goal. If it advanced John's career it was good; if it hurt him it was bad. If she had to be insincere, a bit manipulative from time to time, if she had to scheme against their enemies, it was all justified by the larger good. Mila Mulroney displays that same core of certainty. For both women, for any successful political wife, self-doubt is a foreign concept.

Just as Olive accepted the rightness of her own mission, she accepted, apparently without question, the limitations the fifties and political life placed on women. She hid her stainless-steel determination behind a demure modesty, and her bitterness behind a sweet smile. Her ambitions weren't ideological per se — she had no social strategy or economic plan for the masses. Like her husband, like every politician, she was powerfully attracted to power itself.

SEVEN

A
commendable failure

THE WRY WIT OF MARYON PEARSON

"Behind every successful man stands a surprised woman."

attributed to Maryon Pearson by her husband, Mike,
in volume I of his memoirs, 1972

IF OLIVE DIEFENBAKER WAS A creamy unguent that soothed and lubricated political life in the capital, Maryon Pearson was a splash of astringent right in the eye. An irreverent and very knowing observer of the political scene, Maryon's arch sense of humour was a delightful personal characteristic but, more than once, an embarrassing political liability. Reproduced in newsprint, her wry asides sounded acidic, and she soon developed a national reputation for being standoffish and remote. As Peter Newman wrote in *The Distemper of our Times*, published in 1968:

> Shy and stiff in public, clinging to her dark glasses when seated on the speakers' platform, [Maryon Pearson] was the possessor of a manner too tart for the cautious clichés of Canadian politics.

Political wives are not meant to be tart, in any sense of the word. Nor are they encouraged to be forthright. Yet Maryon Pearson made little effort to disguise her contempt for most aspects of public life during her decade in Ottawa. She once described the central drama of life in the capital, the daily Question Period in the House of Commons, as "boring and frustrating." That is exactly what it often is, of course. Maryon should have been commended for her restraint.

Instead, acerbic remarks like those sent nervous women's editors scurrying for euphemisms. ("A very private person," was a favourite.) On the rare occasions when she met the press, Maryon apparently couldn't help answering questions honestly — and often amusingly.

One story, recounted in all the various biographical accounts of Maryon and in her own husband's memoirs, perfectly illustrates her approach to political life and her subversive wit. At the end of a long day, after a tiring meeting in Mike Pearson's adopted riding of Algoma East, those attending were asked if they had anything else to bring up. "Yes," replied Maryon, not missing a beat. "About twelve cups of coffee and eight donuts."

Someone should design a poster depicting Maryon Pearson as an early hero of the feminist resistance, an *agent provocateur* wearing a single strand of pearls, determined to undermine and expose the hypocrisy and banality of Canadian public life. The poster would be black and white; Maryon would be wearing sunglasses and holding a black cigarette holder trailing smoke in the shape of a question mark. Contemporary feminists would stick it right on their walls alongside their lifesize photos of Cyndi Lauper and Lily Tomlin. It would be subtitled: Signs of Intelligent Life in the Universe.

Not that the well brought-up doctor's daughter from Winnipeg saw herself as a feminist guerrilla or any kind of rebel. Nor is there any trace of personal political ambition in the few interviews Maryon gave, or in her conduct. Unlike Olive Diefenbaker she did not behave like a perennial campaign manager for her husband. She liked family life, loved being a grandmother, cherished her privacy and most of the time tried to avoid the false clatter of politics. It was only her funny asides and her ill-concealed impatience with cant that mark her as one of the most trenchant and interesting of Canada's political wives — even if, or maybe because, she was also one of the most unwilling. Maryon was about as subversive as a wife could be in the early sixties. She must have been a welcome antidote to the excessive sweetness of Olive Diefenbaker and the saintliness of her other contemporary, the governor general's wife, Madame Georges Vanier, a woman who was almost beatified in her own time. Compared to those two, Maryon cleansed the nation's palate like a vinegary salad — whether the nation liked it or not.

Friends describe the private Maryon Pearson as warm, witty and intellectually alive — very different from the shy, diffident public figure. Diplomat and diarist Charles Ritchie, himself one of the keenest observers of our political life, said Maryon was, "very funny and very much on the mark in her comments." But Maryon wanted to keep the joke *en famille*. There is no evidence that she yearned to have microphones thrust in her face, entertain lady journalists hungry for insights on menu planning or have unflattering closeups of herself appear regularly in leading newspapers — all routine indignities for truly ambitious political wives.

Unlike Olive or Mila or other women who marry ready-made politicians and are eager for the lifestyle that entails, Maryon, in 1928, married a likeable young academic with no visible appetite for politics. Lester Pearson was a history professor at the University of Toronto and she was his student, many years his junior. His only secret vice was sports, and Maryon worried that he would throw over a promising academic career to become a fulltime hockey or football coach. Lester Pearson was not a man who, as Jean Chrétien used to say mockingly of Joe Clark, had "an appointment with destiny." Pearson's son, Geoffrey, said once in an interview that his father didn't even consider becoming prime minister until 1956, only a few years before he won the job. As it was, Pearson only became a cabinet minister through an unusual and unplanned series of events. He was a promising diplomat with the External Affairs Department in 1956 when he was seconded by Prime Minister Louis St. Laurent to serve in cabinet as minister of external affairs. Once in cabinet, Pearson was obliged by democratic etiquette to run for a seat, to abandon the carpeted corridors of diplomacy for the noisy cafeteria of politics. Reluctantly, and with occasional bad grace, Maryon followed. It wasn't the life she wanted.

Eventually Pearson was chosen to lead the Liberal party, but he was in no immediate danger of becoming prime minister in his early days, especially after the Diefenbaker sweep of 1957, which shook the apparently invincible Liberal party to its core. For Maryon, watching results of that devastating election on television, there was a double blow. "We've lost everything," she said to Mike. "We even won our seat."

Despite her dislike of political life, Maryon gamely campaigned for her husband, trying, without much success, to overcome her fear of large crowds. She was comfortable with smaller groups, and particularly among the down-to-earth voters in Pearson's northern Ontario riding of Algoma East. Almost anywhere else she was plainly ill at ease. She once said of campaigning: "I don't know any wife who likes it." She never learned to dissemble, to smile in the face of incredible boredom, to tell the small, fluid lies that are the currency of political life. Asked how she liked the Prairies on one campaign trip out west, she replied: "I prefer the climate on the coast."

She was a bit like Geills Turner in that way, although Geills has far more social confidence. Both women were well-educated Winnipegers from upper-class backgrounds with very limited patience for the political game, but a keen curiosity about politics itself. Both were intelligent and critical. But while Geills is glamorous and vibrates with wholesome good health, Maryon always looked a little strained, tired, even distracted, a condition that became more obvious as her husband's political fortunes deteriorated. On the other hand, Geills is known for aiming her barbs at unsuspecting sales clerks and other lesser mortals from time to time, but there was nothing imperious about Maryon.

Face to face, according to journalist Christina McCall Newman, Maryon's wisecracks didn't sound as bald and aggressive as they looked on the page. "She says things in a slow drawl, that takes much of the sting from their meaning," McCall Newman reported in a 1964 *Maclean's* piece. A friend described Maryon's humour as rueful rather than sarcastic. For example, when the Pearsons were campaigning in London, Ontario, in 1965, a hotel put up a sign saying "Welcome to Liberace and to the Prime Minister." Maryon joked to her husband, "Second fiddle to a piano player." The next day, so the story goes, the sign was changed to read, "Welcome Mrs. Pearson and husband."

In 1963 Pearson was finally elected prime minister, and he and his wife moved into 24 Sussex. During Mike's first term as leader of the Opposition, Maryon had time for her own pursuits, for her reading and cooking and for her friends. She even took up painting. All that ended when the couple moved a few blocks from the leader of the Opposition's official residence, Stornoway, to Sussex Drive. Living in the elegant stone mansion overlooking the Ottawa River was, said Maryon, "a bit like living in a hotel." As she told interviewer McCall Newman in 1964, after several months as wife of the prime minister:

> I miss Stornoway. That really seemed like our house. I did the cooking and some of the gardening. Now I don't cook at all. I even miss going to the supermarket, and pushing a cart around. Oh, and all the normal things like being able to go without a hat.

She also missed her weekly bridge game with friends.

> There are so many places I have to go. All the diplomatic corps wives want to give lunches for me — this week it's the Turks and last week it was the Dutch and the Poles. And then people keep wanting me to open things. I won't go to bazaars because if you open one, you never stop. But if there is an antique show or craft exhibit I feel I ought to be there.

In Maryon's day being a fulltime housewife was a perfectly respectable occupation, even for a woman whose kids had grown up and left home. But she was expected to earn her keep by "entertaining" for her husband, by wooing and flattering people who might be useful to his career. Maryon was not a recluse or a stay-at-home housewife like Jeanne St. Laurent, who took refuge from public life in her Quebec City kitchen, but she was no party girl either. She avoided the mega-teas that Olive Diefenbaker loved, but she couldn't escape social life entirely. As a diplomatic wife in the forties, she formed the Ottawa Dance Club, a social group open to all diplomatic ranks. The club was an alternative to the formal diplomatic parties from which second secretaries and the lower ranks were excluded, and Maryon, like Maureen McTeer twenty years later, enthusiastically supported any attempt to make diplomatic life more egalitarian. When she was comfortable with her guests she could be an interesting host. At one party for someone on Pearson's staff, Maryon pinned up cartoons from the *New Yorker* magazine around the dining room at 24 Sussex and got guests to try to identify themselves in the caricatures.

If she was still alive now she'd probably have a bumper sticker on her car: I'd rather be reading. Maryon read widely, both history — which she studied at university — and literature. She admitted, with some chagrin, to being a fan of Edna St. Vincent Millay, Katherine Mansfield (back in fashion in the eighties) and Scottish novelist Muriel Spark, but she hastened to tell an interviewer she also read serious things, too. Maryon also confessed to being "terribly interested" in politics. However she didn't consider what went on every day in the House of Commons as politics — certainly not politics at its most edifying. Unlike Olive, who frequently watched proceedings from the visitors' gallery, Maryon was like the modern wives — Maureen, Mila and Geills — who rarely show up on Parliament Hill. (Nowadays, however, they don't have to since Question Period is televised.) "I feel that they're frittering away hours in meaningless haranguing when they should be getting important things accomplished," Maryon once said of the Commons. She added:

> Then I get furious when the government is under attack — my boiling point is low. I'd sooner be at home doing things I like. I don't ever seem to have enough time to read, and I love to read.

For her "cause" — a sort of Lenten duty for all political spouses — Maryon promoted Canadian artists and artisans. In the mid-sixties there was none of the market research and political brainstorming that goes on today when it comes to choosing an appropriate charity for the first lady. Those were simpler times. Within limits, political wives were free to choose their own good deeds. Maryon's enthusiasm for Canadian art actually predated her time in public life. When the Pearsons lived at 24 Sussex, Maryon made sure a catholic selection of Canadian art decorated the walls. In one of her few overtures to the media, she invited reporters to 24 Sussex while Mike was prime minister for the unveiling of her Canadiana collection of pioneer furniture and art, arranged with due respect for historical authenticity, in a basement room.

While Maryon was making these modest efforts, Jackie Kennedy was renovating the entire White House and the common perception of political wife. It was Maryon's misfortune to overlap with the most glamorous American political wife of the century. When the Kennedys visited Ottawa in the early sixties, at the peak of their popularity, poor Maryon stood stiffly in the background looking very old and a little dowdy. It was "My American Cousin" all over again, all those white Kennedy teeth and that tall, elegant woman next to a rather folksy, frumpish and short Canadian couple. (And Mike with a bow-tie, yet.) Maryon was probably the intellectual equal of Jackie Kennedy and could undoubtedly hold her own in a conversation. But that isn't the way women are measured, and it certainly wasn't the way political wives were measured — especially not post-Jackie. After the Kennedys, wives almost had an obligation to the glamorous.

Despite the fact that Maryon was socially awkward, she made important behind-the-scenes contributions to the nation's political life in the form of pointed advice and pungent asides she directed at her husband. The Pearsons were a close couple and he was said to be delighted by her sense of humour, even if his political managers weren't. If he didn't always agree with her advice, he apparently welcomed it — and he could count on it to be honest. As secretary of state in 1955, Pearson commented that Canadian-US relations were like living with a wife. "Sometimes it is difficult and even irritating to live with her, but it is always impossible to live without her." Judy Lamarsh, the former Liberal cabinet minister and one of the country's first prominent female politicians, credited Maryon Pearson with encouraging Mike to establish a royal commission on the status of women. "I think Maryon was pretty liberal on the subject," Lamarsh recalled in an interview she gave before her death.

There were other flickerings of a feminist consciousness — or at least an awareness of the importance of an independent identity for women. In the interview with *Maclean's* in 1964, Maryon said she regretted not having worked after college. "Now I often do wish that I'd had a job for a while. I think women should work and I hoped my daughter would have a career." (Instead, her daughter married a doctor immediately after college and had five children.)

In our eagerness to reset recorded history to a feminist beat, we have to beware of wishful thinking. Maryon resisted the more demeaning and humiliating aspects of being a political wife, but she also did what she was told when she feared her husband might be hurt. "I married him for better or for worse, not just for lunch," she said in 1967. In many ways, theirs was a conventional, patriarchal relationship: he was years older than Maryon, and when they married she immediately abandoned any notion of beginning a career of her own, to devote herself to his. In some ways Pearson was an unlikely patriarch, with his goofy lisp and his affable, hands-in-the-pocket manner. He clearly respected his wife's opinions yet he was infected with the usual male chauvinism of his era — he very much saw Judy Lamarsh, for example, as a token woman politician. In 1976, Judy told an interviewer that when Pauline Jewett, then a Liberal, asked Pearson for a cabinet seat, he replied: "We've already got one woman cabinet minister!"

Maryon was quick to resign from the Voice of Women, a liberal, anti-war organization in 1963, when it became apparent that VOW's opposition to nuclear arms on Canadian soil was at odds with freshly minted Liberal policy. Maryon said VOW had become "much more belligerent" on the nuclear question since she joined, an accusation that was refuted by the president and later senator, Therese Casgrain. What really happened was that Mike Pearson bowed to American pressure and agreed to let Canada's planes carry nuclear warheads — and Maryon was forced to fall into line, whatever her private thoughts.

It wasn't the only time Mrs. Pearson sacrificed her own interests for her husband's career. When London was bombarded during the Second World War she wanted to stay with Mike, who was working at Canada's High Commission in the English capital at the time. She and some other Canadian political wives had become very involved as volunteers in "the war effort," and appeared to be having the time of their lives. But Pearson insisted Maryon return to Winnipeg to be with their children and she did, after heated arguments. She later said, wistfully, that she loved London because it, "allows you a life of your own."

Whether she was bitter about these sacrifices is hard to judge from the public record. In 1962 she told a reporter:

> Men are strange about politics. I have been around the world twice and know politicians from many cultures. They are all alike. As long as they find themselves in the middle of it, they say they are sorry that all their time is taken up by politics. But as soon as they have lost and are out — Oh, how terrible for them!

For all the mockery in that statement, she was very protective of her husband and impatient with his critics. She chided reporters covering the Pearsons' trip to London in 1966:

> The newspapers are always at the poor old prime minister — it seems he can never do anything right. Sometimes I think how marvellous it would be to get all the newspaper editors together to form a cabinet and see how they could run the country.

On the other hand, Maryon appeared quite sanguine about her own public image. As she told the *Vancouver Sun* in 1965: "I may be a little shy and I'm afraid I'm not very outgoing, but I've never considered myself misunderstood."

In 1968, when the Pearsons were leaving public life, a Liberal women's group made a presentation to Maryon. Afterwards, she gave what her husband described as her first speech (a line he used more than once).

"Thank you and *merci*," was all she said. It was all she ever said. Later, in an unusual scrum, she told reporters: "I know what you're going to ask me: What did I like about being a prime minister's wife, what didn't I like. I could do the interview myself." Cracked Mike: "I can tell you what she liked least: Being interviewed."

When her husband retired in 1968, Maryon Pearson said goodbye to public life with no regrets. After he died in 1976 she dropped from view. There were always rumours about Maryon in Ottawa — rumours that she was an unhappy, troubled person who suffered from a disabling shyness — but if she did have problems she would never have aired them publicly. When she became a political wife, she didn't hand herself over, body and soul, to her husband's political handlers in the current style. Instead, Maryon tried to live her life as privately and normally as possible.

Surprisingly, she did submit to a short interview with the *Toronto Sun* in March 1977. She told the newspaper she felt sorry for Margaret Trudeau, who was then at the height of her notoriety. Maryon said that during her five years at 24 Sussex (1963–1967) she purposely ducked the press. "But I was much older," she continued. "Mrs. Trudeau's very young and inexperienced. I'm very upset by what's happening to her, but I think that if she wants a private life, it's not a good idea to talk to the press."

What Maryon may not have realized is that the modern political wife can't get away with hiding behind dark glasses and keeping the press at bay with caustic one-liners. She is under enormous pressure these days to do much more than just the minimum. Pouring tea and throwing a few afternoon cocktail parties isn't enough. She is required to devote all her energy, time and intelligence to the party. Charm is an invaluable political commodity, and beauty is a proven attention-getter and both are largely the province of the wife. The more she looks and behaves like a slender, young airline stewardess, the better. Middle-aged housewives need not apply.

Maryon concluded her musings about Margaret with the *Toronto Sun*: "If she [Margaret] asked for my advice, I'd be happy to give it to her. But she hasn't, and I don't intend to transmit it through the press." Then she caught herself: "Look at me, here I am talking to the press myself."

What a shame she didn't do it more often. The unvarnished, astute and politically subversive memoirs of political wives like Maryon Pearson would be so much more interesting than the sanitized self-justifications of their husbands. And, with Maryon at least, vastly more amusing.

EIGHT

*L*iving with conflict

MARRYING A POLITICIAN IS SOMETIMES A MATTER OF BLIND TRUST

"One person should not be held responsible for the other. Two married persons have their own identity and they must have the opportunity to pursue their own activities."

JEANNE SAUVÉ, 1974

JEANNE SAUVÉ WAS A CABINET minister when she made the remarks quoted above, and the wife of a former cabinet minister, a woman who has seen conflict of interest from all possible angles. As governor general she was embarrassed a few years ago by the disclosure that her husband, Maurice, was a member of an organization that promotes trade between Canada and South Africa. Maurice resigned, repudiated the pro-apartheid remarks of the group's chairman and faded back into comfortable anonymity. But the incident revived all the difficult and sensitive questions about conflict of interest, about how much one spouse should be held accountable for the crimes, indiscretions and associations of the other. In 1974, when she was in cabinet, it was clear where Sauvé stood. "Times have changed and women must be allowed to take up careers," she said. "The concept of Caesar's wife is a base cliché that leads to the enslavement of women."

It is hard to argue with that. Wives or spouses should be free to pursue their own careers, hold their own opinions, join their own associations without fear of damaging their political partner's job prospects. But where to draw the line? Should Maureen McTeer be applauded or repudiated for lending her name and her national celebrity, a celebrity she initially won through marriage rather than accomplishment, to the pro-choice movement? What if Mila or, less improbably, Lillian Vander Zalm, decided to actively support REAL Women? Would *that* be all right? Would it have been proper for Maurice Sauvé, a private citizen, to continue his membership in the pro-apartheid group or was he compelled to resign? Should Geraldine Ferraro's campaign for vice-president of the United States have been derailed by revelations about her husband's private business dealings?

As long as they aren't using their connection with government to get funding, political spouses should be free to join any organizations they wish, hold any views they wish — and let the political chips fall where they may. If their association with REAL Women, or a militant sect of the animal liberation movement, or the Knights of Columbus becomes public, it is another fact for voters to applaud, dismiss or remember on election day. Because while political spouses have a right to an independent life, they don't operate in a vacuum; their activities do have an effect on the public perception of their partner.

Maureen McTeer's pro-choice stand tells us something about Joe Clark, and for those who agree with and admire Maureen McTeer it tells us good things. We all make judgments about people based on whom they marry. Their choice tells us something about what they admire, what they want, what they will tolerate. However, it doesn't tell us the whole story. For instance, there is nothing in Jeanne Sauvé's history, speeches or behavior to suggest that she is a supporter of the South African regime, notwithstanding her husband's former associations. Spouses aren't mirror images of one another in politics any more than in real life. Nor does Joe Clark's liberal-mindedness on the abortion issue mark him as a "liberal" in other areas, like our relations with the Soviet Union, where the external affairs minister betrays a simple-minded, reflexive anti-Communism worthy of the Reagan White House.

In this murky area there is one clear rule: political spouses should not exploit their partners' positions for their own financial or business gain. It may seem like an easy rule to enforce, but is it? Some say that in this country, with its relatively small business and legal elite, conflict of interest is inevitable. Paths cross constantly and particularly in the world of big business, government is involved in every deal. For a couple — one partner in politics and one in business — to remain chaste in such a milieu is impossible, goes the argument. (That has certainly been the case with the Mulroney government, which has spawned a whole sub-genre of political reporting devoted entirely to ferreting out cousins, brothers and cronies of cabinet ministers who are somehow on the take.) Various attempts by successive governments to solve this problem over the last decade, have ended in confusion and paralysis.

In 1979 Joe Clark tried to introduce a strict new conflict code which stipulated that cabinet ministers' spouses had to put all their holdings, outside of personal savings and their homes, into a blind trust. There was to be no hint that cabinet wives might be making small personal fortunes on the side because of insider information, or covertly managing their husbands' businesses for them. Clark adopted the scorched-earth solution, the purist approach: don't just prohibit sin, remove the occasion of sin. The opposition came from an unlikely place — Jane Crosbie, the lively, funny and very astute wife of

Newfoundland cabinet minister John Crosbie. Jane had 2,800 dollars tucked away in stocks, money she'd saved from groceries over the years, money that belonged to her, and she was damned if Joe Clark was going to tell her what to do with it. "I couldn't believe it," Jane recalled later. "Here I was, strictly a housewife, not a politician. Why should I have to put my savings in a blind trust?"

Jane Crosbie had a point and her impromptu rebellion provoked an outpouring of support from across the country. Joe's ambitious code eventually died with his government in 1980. But the questions raised by the Noreen Stevens case six years later aren't as easy to resolve. Noreen Stevens, wife of the former minister for regional and industrial expansion, Sinclair Stevens, is a pioneer, one of the first female graduates of Osgoode Hall in 1959, one of the few cabinet wives actively involved in big business. She has another kind of fame, too, as the first modern-day political wife at the centre of a conflict-of-interest investigation.

Noreen was a long-time partner in her husband's various financial adventures, and when Sinc went into politics fulltime in 1972 she took over management of the family real-estate business. It was much later, when she tried to negotiate a 2.6 million-dollar loan for those businesses with a man who had extensive dealings with her husband's government department, that the Stevens got into hot water. We are not talking about grocery money and we are not talking about a housewife.

As I write this, the Parker committee of inquiry set up to probe the Stevens case has not yet reported and we have no idea how the Mulroney government is going to respond. At present, there is no requirement for wives and families of cabinet ministers to disclose their holdings or put them in blind trusts. In a way, it is a feminist model: the rules treat spouses as independent persons, not chattels. Indeed, the Stevens case flushed out some unlikely feminists, not the least of whom was Noreen's husband of twenty-eight years. Sinc Stevens, who was forced to resign from cabinet as a result of the scandal, scolded the Parker inquiry: "If my wife was a man, you wouldn't be asking these questions." That noted feminist and progressive, former deputy-prime minister Erik Nielsen, even charged the opposition with attacking female entrepreneurialship.

Typically, Nielsen was distorting the picture. The Stevens case wasn't about sexism, it was about the propriety of one spouse doing business with a man who had dealings with her husband's government department. In this case, the spouse in business happened to be a woman. But it can and has happened the other way. In Ontario, cabinet minister Elinor Caplan was forced to resign when questions were raised about some government contracts her husband landed. Both situations raise difficult questions for couples in "mixed marriages." How much of their daily business can they discuss with one another? How much can they avoid sharing without damaging their marriage? Noreen Stevens says she never discussed the 2.6 million-dollar loan she needed to save the family business with her husband. A remarkable display of discretion, but is it realistic to expect every couple to be that careful? Or should the non-political spouse, male or female, sacrifice an independent career in business so that there won't be even a hint of scandal?

The Americans rely more on disclosure than prohibition to deal with conflict of interest. In other words, political spouses can do what they want as long as the public is fully aware of what they are up to. This theory rests on a belief in the cleansing nature of publicity, and is much in vogue in British Columbia these days where conflict of interest isn't so much a problem as a way of life for BC Premier Bill Vander Zalm. When the former tulip bulb mogul became premier in 1985, he mused about getting rid of the family business, his Fantasy Garden World tourist park in Richmond, BC. But once elected, Vander Zalm decided he didn't want to sell the place after all. His wife, Lillian, was too sentimentally attached to it. So he made her president of the holding company and his daughter, Juanita, vice-president, and when he can get away from the premier's office, Bill pitches in, too. He and Lillian live in a mock-historic castle on the Fantasy Garden site and Bill has been known to have the whole cabinet over for special meetings. He says there is no conflict of interest because Lillian lets them use the castle for free. Once again reality outdoes satire in BC.

Vander Zalm doesn't even pretend there is any arm's-length relationship involved. "Let's face it," he once told reporters, "man and wife are one, so we're together on it. . . . " The gardens have benefited more than once from provincial actions — notably a rezoning from agricultural land that added a couple of million to the value of the premier's family business — but neither zoning, nor height regulations, nor public opinion can thwart the relentless march of capitalism in BC.

Maybe there are two answers to conflict of interest: a strict code governing financial conflicts and total freedom for spouses when it comes to personal opinion. Maryon Pearson should not have been forced to resign from the liberal, pacifist Voice of Women in the mid-sixties because the organization vehemently opposed her husband's pro-nuclear foreign policy. Maureen McTeer had every right to speak out on abortion twenty years later. Margaret Trudeau was within her rights, too, when she was promoting her latest spiritual insight in the seventies. Eleanor Roosevelt has been nearly beatified in recent years for her forceful speeches on social justice, yet she was widely criticized in her own time. Why did Betty Ford face censure for speculating frankly on the sexual behavior of her children? Political wives should not be expected to forfeit all rights to independent opinion, and political parties and the public should stop asking them to act like tame parrots.

On the other hand, there should be strict rules prohibiting the spouse (and close relatives) of a politician from doing business of any kind with government. Perhaps the government will resurrect Joe Clark's strict 1979 code. Some say this will discourage bright, ambitious two-career couples from entering politics and leave the field open to traditional patriarchs with stay-at-home wives, along with a smattering of widows and divorced women — in other words, the same gang that runs things today. It is said that strict conflict-of-interest rules will particularly discourage married women from entering politics. How many husbands would give up their careers, their outside interests, their independence of mind and their economic security for their wives' careers? As it is, few men will make the sacrifices that are routinely expected of political wives. That is partly why most women in politics are divorced, widowed or single. There are hardly any married women politicians in their twenties or thirties in Ottawa and only a smattering in various political legislatures. Child rearing is one explanation and difficulties in raising money another, but so is the distinct shortage of male political wives.

Liberal MP Sheila Copps is an exception in this area, as in many. Her husband, American Ric Marrero, the television cameraman she met on a southern vacation, tends to keep out of the limelight, and he isn't rich, powerful or well-connected enough to pose any serious conflict of interest for his wife. Despite that, Marrero got a rude introduction to public life when it was revealed that he was having trouble with immigration because of a couple of minor drug convictions. Ever since, Tory MPs — and the prime minister — never miss a chance to aim drug-related jokes at Copps, one of their favourite targets in the House of Commons.

More common among political husbands are the Denis Thatchers: florid old gentlemen, happy with their directorships, their gardening and their clubs. They may be quaint, but they aren't always harmless. Denis has caused Maggie some discomfort (if no discernible political damage) because of his doughty right-wing notions and his extensive business interests in South Africa. As Geraldine Ferraro discovered it is probably safest to have no husband at all.

Somehow that isn't a satisfactory solution to the problem of conflict of interest or to the shortage of women in public life. Who wants a Parliament open only to women without husbands and men who are married to airheads? On the other hand, it is nonsense to argue that strict conflict-of-interest rules will eliminate "the best people" from running, as if succeeding on Bay Street is a measure of moral virtue. Maybe our public life is already too dominated by business people and lawyers. Making politics less congenial for people in those professions with a strict conflict code may clear the way for more schoolteachers, public health nurses, academics and cashiers to run for Parliament. Unlike business and law, those aren't male-dominated professions. If the pin-striped brigade abandons political power for the private sector, there will be other groups ready to take their turn in Ottawa. By casting a wider net, we will land more women as candidates, not as wives. So strict conflict rules could actually increase the number of women in the Commons and at the same time elevate the moral tone. The two may not be unconnected.

NINE

Alternate wifestyles

GEILLS TURNER, SHELLEY PETERSON,
LILLIAN VANDER ZALM AND LUCILLE
BROADBENT TRY SOME SUBTLE
ALTERATIONS

"I am not the same as Mila; she has her style and I have mine, and I think there is room for both."

SHELLEY PETERSON

IN THE UNITED STATES THE political landscape is changing in a profound but still almost unrecognized way; more and more leading congressmen and senators, among them presidential hopefuls, have wives with real jobs. Some of these wives even have jobs that overlap with the world of politics. A leading Republican contender for the presidency, Senator Bob Dole, is married to Elizabeth Dole, the secretary of transport in Reagan's cabinet. Democratic party contenders Mike Dukasis (the governor of Massachusetts) and Bruce Babbitt, the former governor of Arizona, have wives in business and law respectively. Democratic Senator Paul Simon's wife is an author and arms-control activist. How many of these women — and the generation they represent — are going to be content with life as a full-time shopper?

It should make for interesting election campaigns: a solitary candidate making his lonely way across the country with only four hundred media, three hundred advisers and 150 technicians for company and support. Meanwhile, in an unprecedented display of self-assertion, his wife peers into a microscope in some distant lab, selfishly absorbed in a quixotic quest for a cure for cancer, unapologetically uninvolved in her husband's campaign. How will the political culture survive without a wife to soothe the political waters, divert and distract photographers, accept the bouquets, repair the candidate's frayed ego after every poll or dash into a washroom in order to remove coffee stains from his trousers?

The questions aren't quite as pressing in Canada, where change is a slower and less certain thing. The two most likely successors to Mila Mulroney — Geills Turner and Lucille Broadbent — are very much products of the current system, wives who played on farm teams for twenty years. Neither would be quite as wifely as Mila, but it is doubtful that either will seriously challenge or — even more daring — refuse the role of political wife. On Parliament Hill, which lags seriously behind the rest of the country in almost every area of social intercourse, two-career marriages are still relatively rare. Most cabinet ministers' wives devote all their time to their husbands' careers, keep house, run the constituency office or discreetly hold down jobs that have nothing to do with politics. Except for Maureen McTeer, Noreen Stevens and the irrepressible Jane Crosbie, they stay out of the public eye.

If there is a new generation of wives coming, it is in the provinces, not in Ottawa. To track new political styles these days you need look no further than Queen's Park. Long before the startling revelation that Brian Mulroney knows how to change his son Nicolas' diapers, Ontario Premier David Peterson was routinely spending "quality time" with his three kids and the family dog, endearingly named Blueberry Muffin. There were pictures in national magazines of the soon-to-be premier acting as caregiver while his wife, Shelley, an actress, was out working.

If her press clippings are to be believed, Shelley Peterson has Mila's fashionable good looks, Maureen McTeer's independent identity and Olive Diefenbaker's diplomacy. In fact, the premier's wife is an interesting combination of Mila and Maureen: she maintains an independent career but also does political duty with her husband from time to time. In her case, her career — she's a professional actress — helps rather than hinders her in the political role. (And perhaps, vice versa. Being the premier's wife guarantees a certain name recognition, at the least.) Acting can be a useful background for politics, as Nancy Reagan has shown, but it is also a glamorous, politically attractive career for the contemporary urban wife — provided she avoids porn and politics. Even post-Bill Davis, Ontario is not ready for Koo Stark, the soft-porn star who sullied Prince Andrew's spotless reputation — or was it the other way around? In any event, the question will likely never arise with the Petersons, neither of whom have put a foot wrong yet.

The riskiest project Shelley has undertaken is a role in a new television sitcom about life in Ottawa in which she plays a female assistant deputy minister. (The sitcom isn't really risky, just a gentle spoof of life in Ottawa, but not something you'd expect Mila Mulroney, for instance, to take part in.) In real life, Shelley is part of the Peterson package around election time, then reverts to regular life between campaigns. But if campaign and career came into conflict, it is by no means certain she would drop a promising dramatic role for the profoundly less satisfying role of political wife. Nor is it certain that her husband would ask her to make that sacrifice. Among other things, he is canny enough to recognize the appeal to a certain kind of voter of a wife who has a mind and life of her own.

Not that Shelley Peterson has turned her back on the traditional wife role. She still does wifely things, like sitting through her husband's dull dinner speeches, being photographed with adorable children, attending party conventions. She comes from a Conservative, upper-middle class professional family in London, Ontario, a family with a keen interest in politics. That may be where she developed her diplomatic skills. Asked once about Mila, she replied carefully, "I am not the same as Mila; she has her style and I have mine, and I think there is room for both." Spoken like a true political wife.

If the Petersons move to Ottawa some day — many see David Peterson as a future prime minister — Shelley's experiment with independence will be tested. The demands on the wife of a prime minister are greater than the demands on a premier's wife, and Ottawa is far stuffier and less tolerant of deviation from tradition than even Toronto. So far, Shelley has lived her own life by quietly insisting on it, not by making unequivocal declarations. She isn't a feminist in the way Maureen McTeer is, but neither is she the compleat corporate wife. She's a wuppie (wife of a young, upwardly mobile, etc., etc., etc.) in the city that yuppies built. Can she continue her career if her husband becomes prime minister? There is no reason why not — although the best dramatic performances in Ottawa generally take place on the floor of the House of Commons. But will she?

The province of British Columbia has always been a little different and Lillian Vander Zalm is a case in point. In some ways, she is the traditional political wife, bouncing along beside her husband on the campaign trail, beaming furiously at potential supporters, full of the same kind of verve and infectious energy that makes Jane Crosbie so popular. (Lillian was such a hit in the last campaign, people started sporting "Lillian for Premier" buttons.) Bill Vander Zalm is also a traditional husband. Actually, that is being kind. Vander Zalm's notions about women don't appear to have evolved beyond the Old Testament. He applauded the election of women in the last provincial campaign because "they would certainly dress up the cabinet room and make for better decor." Earlier during the campaign, we got another glimpse of the Vander Zalm marriage. Asked about Lillian's failure to appear at a rally, the Zalm replied: "I ran out of socks and I have no shirts. So we had to get caught up." Pressed to explain he said he would do the laundry himself if he had time — but he would never get it as clean as Lillian. (Bet you haven't heard that one in a long time.)

That's one part of the story. The other is that the Vander Zalms are a happy, well-matched couple who have worked shoulder to shoulder (literally; both are tall, handsome and healthy looking) building a tulip and tourist empire. Dynasty, actually. The Vander Zalms also have four handsome children involved in their business, two sons and two daughters, whose flashing teeth and healthy good looks call to mind the Osmond family.

The Vander Zalms, conservative Roman Catholics, are firm believers in the triple-H version of family trumpeted by the Christian right: heirarchical, heterosexual and holy. In some ways they resemble Jimmy and Tammy Faye Bakker, the recently disgraced TV evangelists. They have the same made-for-television optimism, the same dazzling smiles and they even run a theme park, Fantasy Garden World in Richmond, BC, that is a modest version of the Bakker's Heritage USA religious theme park. There is a strength in that kind of marriage, in that type of partnership, although as the Bakkers discovered, it provides no protection against the sins of the world.

You could call this phenomenon the Public Couple: a commercial and personal arrangement aimed at promoting not just two individuals, but also the relationship between them. A specialized sub-species is the Political Couple, of whom Nancy and Ronnie are best known. Brian and Mila are a Political Couple, too, as were Ferdinand and Imelda Marcos, and Evita and Juan Peron. In the usual Political Couple, both partners are exclusively involved in promoting, advancing and protecting the husband's political career. For the Vander Zalms, the inner dynamic is a little different. Lillian has a real job. She brings in the money. She runs the family business, the theme park in Richmond, complete with a castle, flower gardens and a bustling souvenir shop that sells, among other things, Lillian's trademark headband ($5.95). Lillian does not, like Mila and Nancy, spend most of her time puzzling over fabric swatches or personnel problems in her husband's office.

When he became premier, Bill made his wife chief executive officer of Fantasy Garden World, and gave her daily responsibility for running the place while he gets on with the important business of crushing British Columbia's labour movement. But he is still, metaphorically speaking, chairman of the board. He is still in charge and the Vander Zalms make sure their public understands that. During the campaign, when Lillian's mother, Marie Mihalick, criticized Vander Zalm (she said he was a good gardener, "but I don't know if he's going to make a good premier") Lillian immediately sided with her husband. She implied that her mother, a long-time NDP supporter, was a bit dotty. "She was conned," Lillian said. "The NDP told her she was going to a tea party instead of a political rally." A lot of British Columbia voters thought Mrs. Mihalick was uncommonly astute, but the incident made it clear that Lillian's first loyalties are with her husband not her mother. As Lillian told the *Vancouver Sun* in 1986: "I never, ever wanted a career. I like being a mother. I like being a wife. I've never thought of it any other way." So what does she call running a multi-million-dollar business — a hobby?

Despite her unfashionable notions, there is something commendable about Lillian. She came from a large, poor Manitoba family, dropped out of school after grade seven and has worked ceaselessly ever since. She has a confidence and enthusiasm that makes her attractive to voters and to the people she greets daily at her fantasy theme park. But she also comes from a generation of women who believe it is necessary that a wife play down her own talents and abilities — especially if they are considered "male" abilities — lest she overshadow her husband. In the Vander Zalm's fantasy world, Lillian's fame, wealth and success spring from her marriage — or so the story goes. That doesn't mean Lillian's business acumen isn't recognized — it is, both by her husband and his friends. But sadly, Lillian knows her place.

Maybe Geills Turner will be the one to blow the whole system to pieces. She has the personality — tightly coiled, intense, with a reputation for volatility. But does she have the desire? For the last few years, since she was dragged reluctantly back into the limelight from the leafy seclusion of the affluent Toronto neighbourhood of Forest Hill, she has sent out mixed signals. On one hand, Geills loathes the press and avoids publicity. On the other, she is an agile and interesting performer when she wants to be — charming, intelligent and, that most newsworthy of qualities, provocative.

Most people who know her say that Geills will find it hard to play the secondary role required of wives, to be the even-toothed bimbo or the warm, matronly presence. She is too competitive, too self-assured — some say too self-centred — and too imbued with the confidence of class to stifle herself for long. Like the daughter of many successful fathers, she was taught to believe in herself. Her father, David E. Kilgour, chief executive officer of Great-West Life Assurance company in Winnipeg from 1957 to 1971, "respected me as an equal, not as a daughter," Geills once said. Kilgour's bright, athletic daughter is also too well educated to be happy with the intellectual half-life of the Ottawa wife. She studied mathematics and physics at the University of Manitoba and McGill, business administration at Harvard and worked briefly as a computer analyst with IBM in New York and Montreal in the fifties, when most working women were secretaries. By any measure she's over-qualified for the job of wife, however exalted the level.

During the seventies, while John was making an es-timated 450,000 dollars a year in corporate law in To-ronto, Geills dodged both publicity and a fulltime career. Instead, she stayed home with the four Turner children, maintained the plumbing in the family's mansion in Toronto and perfected her tennis game. She still does a rigorous daily workout and dresses impeccably; look-ing as good as she does takes time as well as money. She also studied photography for four years at Ryerson. It sounds like an insubstantial pursuit, but Geills ap-parently took it seriously. She told one interviewer she used to stay up until 4:00 a.m. working on assignments, then be at class for eight o'clock the next morning. She was determined not to be bested by eighteen year olds. Geills even flew up north by herself to take pictures.

Then in 1984, just when she was ready to resume a fulltime career, her husband decided to renew his in-terrupted appointment with destiny. First he won the leadership of the Liberal party, then he was prime min-ister for four months, then leader of the Opposition and now there is some danger that he might become prime minister again.

It is difficult to predict what sort of prime minister's wife Geills Turner would be — her husband wasn't in office long enough last time for anyone to form an impression, and when he was a cabinet minister in the Trudeau government in the early seventies, Geills was pregnant and otherwise preoccupied. However, it is easy to predict that the job will be difficult for her, far more difficult than it is for Mila. For one thing, being a political wife is no undertaking for a Type A personality — it requires too much pointless activity, too much Buddha-like detachment; it rewards appearance rather than accomplishment. For another, Geills seems to hate the media even more passionately than most wives. According to one friend, she didn't talk to the press for twenty years because of one negative story. During the 1984 election campaign, Geills accused the *Globe and Mail*, the CTV Network and Southam News Services of supporting the Tories because all three organizations ran polls that accurately predicted the drubbing her husband was about to receive at the hands of the electorate. Being in politics and hating the media is like working in an abattoir and hating the sight of blood. It is exhausting and ultimately self-defeating. Even if your complaints are justified, the media always gets the last word.

Given her personality and her reputation for a certain *hauteur*, Geills may also find it hard to hold herself to the sanitized generalities expected of wives. During the 1984 campaign she made headlines (another thing a smart wife avoids — pictures yes, headlines no) when she declared herself in favour of a nuclear freeze. Her exact words were: "No serious member of the human race could not be for a nuclear freeze because what we're talking about is the potential annihilation of the whole, entire race." No serious member of the human race maybe, but that doesn't include the Reagan administration. At the time of Geills' remarks, her husband was fighting pressure in his party to declare in favour of a freeze. Turner always likes to order whatever his old pal George Shultz is ordering, and the American secretary of state holds that a freeze would be risky. Our NATO allies might not like it either. Geills later tried to make it clear that there is no real distance between her husband and herself on the issue.

> He's in favour of a freeze. I mean every serious, intelligent human being would be in favour of a freeze. What we're talking about is how to go about achieving it.

A lot of dumb voters never did get it straight. They got the distinct impression that Geills was more dovish — on this issue, at least — than John.

Despite the formidable drawbacks of public life, Geills may be lured off the sidelines by the excitement of the game — and by the fact that she has no other immediate prospects. Since her husband re-entered politics, Geills has been ambivalent about her new celebrity to say the least. It is no secret that she argued against John's return to public life in 1979. A few years later, when Turner finally decided to run for the leadership, Geills still appeared to be lukewarm. In the opening weeks of her husband's first comeback tour she departed on a twenty-day photography shoot in China. Turner showed up at a lot of political events alone; he was still doing so during the summer of 1986, when he travelled the country defending his job. During John's brief tenure as prime minister and his early days in Opposition, Geills spent much of her time in Toronto. Around Ottawa, people wondered absently where she was living, what she was doing and started to forget about her.

Then, during the '84 campaign, someone had the idea of sending her north to campaign on her own. She loved it. She told reporters she much preferred working solo to sitting on a platform behind John listening to the same speech night after night. She didn't miss the daily tussles with the media either, or being bopped on the head by a boom mike. As she told one reporter, "I just get out of the way [when the reporters arrive], because I figure they don't want to talk to wifey."

Up north, campaigning with Liberal candidate Lynda Sorensen in the western Arctic, Geills listened, took notes, avoided specifics and kept out of trouble — much to the relief of her chaperone, Ottawa Valley senator Royce Frith. There were a few negative stories when she failed to show up at some old folks' homes in Toronto, but her brief fling with front-line politicking was largely successful. Senator Keith Davey, then the Liberals' chief strategist, apparently invented the northern tour for Geills to get her out of headquarters where she was driving everyone crazy with her arguments, demands and suggestions. (Given the amateurish and pathetic state of

that campaign, maybe they should have listened to her.)
In his book, *The Rainmaker*, Davey recalls:

> The lady reminds me a little of a rock star — that is,
> when the curtain is up, and she's on stage, she is nothing
> short of magnificent. When the curtain comes down she
> is capable of giving everyone a difficult time. . . .

The tension between political organizers and political
wives is one of the enduring micro-dramas of life in
Ottawa, but Geills' high-handedness exacerbated traditional rivalries. Ironically, the ploy to get her out of
town backfired. Campaigning up north seemed to whet
her appetite — at least temporarily — for the political
arena. She played a more public part in her husband's
second run for the leadership in 1986, especially at the
decisive convention in Ottawa in November, where Geills
was buoyantly present, in the peak of preppie good
health, crackling with energy. There were earlier hints,
too, that Geills would not shun the celebrity and influence that comes with being the prime minister's wife.
"There is a lot of power in the role of political wife, and
I'd like to do something positive with it," she mused in
one interview. In another, she said:

> Hopefully, I'm enough older than Margaret and Mau-
> reen, that it would be easier for me to reconcile the two
> roles [of wife and person] with one foot in each camp.
> I'd like to think I can be a supportive wife, with enough
> independence to make some sort of contribution of my
> own.

She also said she wanted to, "avoid seeming to be interested only in those issues women are interested in. Women also care about unemployment."

In more traditional terms, Geills even spoke sympathetically of her husband's travails. After he won a 76 percent endorsement from his party, Geills told a reporter:

> I'm very happy. Its been a difficult two years. After that kind of defeat [by the Tories in 1984], it takes a lot of strength — which I think my husband has shown in considerable amounts — to pick himself up and go like he has for the last two years. Often, he was alone. People sort of drifted away, saying "Oh, the Liberal party is dead, and we'll go back and do something else."

From someone who often gives the impression that she is indifferent to her husband and his world, it was rare praise. An Ottawa lawyer who worked for Turner, Stuart Langford, once told freelance journalist Charlotte Gray: "John tenses up when she's around because she can be so critical. She rattles him."

If Geills does move into 24 Sussex we can brace ourselves for another round of expensive redecorating. Her tastes run more to Ralph Lauren than to Giovanni Mowinkel, but she and Mila Mulroney have in common a comfortable upper middle-class background, a private school education, intelligence and a deep interest in the surface of things. But there are important differences, too. Geills' ambitions don't appear to be as tied up with her husband's as Mila's are, nor does she have the luxury of waiting to make her mark in life later on, after her husband's career fades. Geills is already in her late forties. Unless she makes her move soon, she will never escape her husband's shadow. Yet she is frustrated by the same limitations and unwritten rules that thwarted Margaret Trudeau, Maryon Pearson, Maureen McTeer. For example, she doesn't want to publish her photography while John is still in politics, as she told one interviewer, "because it would look like I was using him. I would feel paranoid if I thought that my book could not stand on its own merits."

That leaves Geills with one option: be the best political wife she can be. Yet even with her perfectionist personality, it is hard to imagine her devoting herself as fully to the life as Mila. Will she feel obliged to adopt a charity, for instance? As a private citizen she has not conspicuously or actively "done good." In 1984 she was appointed to the board of the Shaw Festival and has been an energetic fundraiser, but that may be considered too highbrow a cause for a prime minister's wife. Somehow posters of limpid-eyed theatre managers asking for life-saving transfusions of cash don't pull at the heart strings. It is equally hard to imagine Geills faking compassion in veterans' hospitals or methodically hugging sick kids. WASPs don't hug. Among other things, they don't like to get wrinkled. Liberal organizers still cringe at the story of Geills turning up at a Toronto food bank with a donation in her Creeds shopping bag. In politics, it isn't the thought that counts — its the packaging.

In summary, it does not look like a happy future for

Geills Turner unless she makes some bold break with tradition and with her own past. She appears to have the ability and drive — the compulsion in fact — to break free. But does she have the courage? "I'm not all that confident," she once told an interviewer. "Confidence only relates to your success." She is not a woman who inspires or encourages sympathy, but there is something poignant in that remark.

For Lucille Broadbent the role is fraught with more danger than it is for Mila or Geills, because there is a certain constituency within the New Democratic Party which repudiates and rejects the traditional wifely role. On the other hand, there are traditionalists — particularly among her husband's trade-union supporters in Oshawa — who would consider it disloyal or questionable if Lucille didn't follow Ed everywhere. So Lucille makes the rounds with her husband, entertains and even campaigns for him in Quebec (she is fluently bilingual) all the while expressing a certain ambivalence about the job and maintaining a certain personal dignity.

A former nurse and schoolteacher, Lucille spent a period of time supporting a child herself and married Ed later in life. "It is very difficult to define the role of the politician's wife," she says. However, a wife must remember that it is the husband who is elected and if the spouse "wants to take a definite position he or she should be elected to a post in the party." Lucille Broadbent would never overstep her bounds and try to direct political strategy the way Olive Diefenbaker did and Mila Mulroney is accused of doing. Neither would she inaugurate another era of gala charity balls. As prime minister's wife she would probably play a minor role, albeit in the traditional way. Whatever her private reservations, she lives and works in the world of real politics. She isn't likely to make any bold declarations of independence from the steps of the Centre Block, however much she may wish to.

Maybe the wife of the future — the new wife, the pro-feminist, not post-feminist wife — will hold one press conference to announce that she will be making no more public appearances, then get on with her job, studies or family and refer all future phonecalls to her husband's office. There are a few brave pioneers who have tried. One is Gayle Morris, a well-respected television reporter on Parliament Hill who happens to be married to New Democratic Party MP Lorne Nystrom. To protect her journalistic reputation, Morris decided, with her husband's agreement, to stop doing political events with Lorne — no more fairs, no speeches, no campaigning in his Saskatchewan riding. To her amusement, her husband was returned to Parliament with an increased majority after the campaign she sat out. Morris says wives can fool themselves into believing they are more important than they are and, in the worst cases, delude themselves into believing that *they* are the politicians. Morris' perfectly sensible approach is considered radical in conservative Ottawa and would be even more revolutionary if her husband held a more prominent position — if, for instance, he became leader of the New Democratic Party. But their experience proves the political structure — and a politician's career — will survive the abdication of a political wife.

The next question for all political couples contemplating a break from tradition is this: will the marriage survive such an abdication?

CONCLUSION

*T*ranscending *wifedom*

POLITICAL WIVES ARE LIKE background music, there and not there. They are usually engaged in purely decorative activities like hugging orphans, descending the steps of airplanes behind their husbands, greeting foreign dignitaries or waving mechanically from a float in the Santa Claus parade. These seem harmless enough pastimes, and that may be why a lot of people don't think very hard or very critically about the long-suffering woman with the strained smile standing slightly behind the candidate, her head tilted at an expectant angle. A lot of people consider political wives amusing anachronisms, historic relics with no bearing on the way modern men and women live their lives. They are so *unnecessary*, these well-dressed women hanging around the fringes of important events with nothing to do but smile mutely and nod sagely. Even their critics don't take them seriously.

I'd be tempted to that view myself, but for my career as a political journalist. I've followed too many wives through too many shopping malls during too many campaigns to regard them as innocent bystanders. Mila doesn't simply trail Brian through throngs of supporters; she works the crowd — bobbing, smiling, waving and periodically casting winning glances in the direction of the ever-present television cameras. Even less cooperative wives — Geills Turner springs to mind — are pressed into service in the struggle to score political points. They are trundled across the country like inanimate props, rolled out onto platforms to smile and wave, then wheeled out a side door, out of reach of the dangerous microphones. God forbid they should blurt out an opinion or deviate in any way from their puppylike devotion to their husband and his political vision. Wives have become the ambitious male politician's most crucial accessory, as important and as trivial as the right tie.

In the spring of 1987 the Reagans and French President François Mitterrand and his wife, Danielle, visited Ottawa within weeks of one another. In both cases, the wives — first Mila and Nancy, then Mila and Danielle — sat together in an attitude of respectful attention while their husbands delivered speeches of surpassing banality to joint sessions of Parliament in Ottawa. Everyone in the crowded chamber — the journalists in the over-hanging gallery, the members of Parliament in their seats, the ambassadors, senators and bureaucrats in the centre aisle — had a legitimate reason to be there. So did the pages and the security guards. Not the wives; their only function was to applaud. They sat at the front of the Commons chamber like handsome but impractical pieces of furniture, visitors from another era.

A political wife has no power of her own, but we shouldn't underestimate the symbolic importance of her role, a role that is implicitly understood but never really examined. The political wife embodies the male political culture's notion of how a wife and, by extension, how women should behave. It is a fanciful notion, as we have seen, with little bearing on the way real men and women live their lives. But it persists for two reasons.

First, wives, at least traditional wives, are useful to the male political culture. They don't merely pack suit-cases and pour tea the way they did in the fifties, they also have a crucial political function, which can best be described as making their husbands seem more human. While her husband declares war, eliminates social ser-vices for the poor or raises taxes, the political wife pats our hand reassuringly and tells us it is all for the best. Her outward display of compassion, her womanly con-cern, provides protective cover for her husband's aggression. Male politicians, the main beneficiaries of this arrangement, are not likely to agitate for change.

As for wives themselves, they are isolated — from their peers, their friends and the rest of society. You can't make a revolution on your own, as Maureen McTeer discovered. Lesser wives are sometimes allowed a degree of anonymity or independence, but not the leading ladies, not front-bench wives. They are still advertisements for a life of service, for a return to a world in which compassion is the exclusive domain of women, and running the world the responsibility of men alone. Maureen McTeer's doggedness and Margaret Trudeau's wacky rebelliousness didn't change a thing. Worse, Mila Mulroney, Nancy Reagan and an upcoming generation of post-feminists are threatening to undo the last decade's small advances. They are turning the traditional, stay-at-home wife into a cult figure, portraying her as a victim of feminist, not masculinist, oppression. There is no revolution, only counter-revolution.

Not all political wives embrace indirect power as avidly as Mila and the post-feminist brigade. Many are victims of a job they didn't define or want. They just happened to marry politicians. Some of them just happened to marry farmers, lawyers or teachers, loving husbands who were apparently innocent of political ambition. As one member of Parliament's wife told me: "You can't always help who you fall in love with — unfortunately." Once in public life, wives discover that they are under house arrest, facing a set of limitations and restrictions that would constitute mental cruelty in more enlightened societies. Yet unless they are married to a strong and secure man, someone who will support them in a small, personal revolution, they are forced to conform. They sacrifice jobs, friends, most outside interests and even family life, for their husband's careers.

In doing so they make themselves vulnerable. They lose their financial independence, their confidence, their old friends, their anonymity and even the right to plan their own leisure hours. Even women married to ordinary members of Parliament complain that their time is not their own; their every waking moment is scheduled for them by their husbands' staffs. If they try to make suggestions, they are told not to interfere, that they have no official role. One wife told me she always wants to tell her husband's officious aides, "Hey, it's my livelihood, too!" Another said, "It is always more stressful to be the passenger than the driver. You have so little control."

This is clearly no job for an adult. How does anyone maintain feelings of self-worth and dignity living entirely for and through someone else? How must it feel to live in a world in which you are "just a wife?" The job is inescapably demeaning, no matter how dignified, self-possessed or intelligent the incumbent — all those wordless smiles, the enforced silence, the lifetime of tagging along. As the public humiliation of Gary Hart's wife, Lee, in May 1987 proved, it can be worse than demeaning; it can be degrading. While her husband told a lie so transparent a six year old could see through it, Lee smiled bravely and said bleakly, "I do not ask Gary what he is doing every moment of his life, nor does he ask me."

It was hard not to wince in pity and embarrassment. It was hard not to be furious, partly at Lee Hart for allowing herself to be used that way, but mostly at the hypocrisy of the political culture. Like all presidential hopefuls, Hart made his family life public property — or at least a sanitized version of his family life. He used his wife and kids on campaign posters and in television ads, in keeping with the North American delusion that being part of a nuclear family automatically bestows moral virtue. Then the press found out about Hart's affair with Donna Rice, a buxom model twenty years his junior. It wasn't only Gary Hart who was exposed as a liar and a hypocrite, but the political milieu that produced him.

Post-feminists applauded Lee Hart rather than feeling sorry for her, on the curious grounds that she and her husband obviously had some kind of businesslike understanding about his sexual wandering. This apparently was the deal: he screws around while she looks the other way and, in return, she gets room and board and proximity to power. Mildred Istona, editor of *Chatelaine*, argued that Lee was not a victim but a canny bargainer. She wrote: "Born too early to have her own career, Lee Hart was politically ambitious and wanted Gary Hart to be president." In other words, she traded off her self-respect for future financial and political gain. You can only marvel at the degree of cynicism about human relationships behind that analysis.

A radical faction of the British Labour party had a novel suggestion a few years ago. It proposed to ban the use of family photographs in campaign literature, on the grounds that such personal information is superfluous, has no political relevance and creates a disadvantage for gays, divorced and single people, anyone who doesn't fit the nuclear mould yet wants to run for public office. It was an idea of such revolutionary potential that it was immediately squashed by the Labour party heirarchy and denounced from every political pulpit in the land. Too bad. It is a provocative and interesting notion, notwithstanding the practical difficulties.

Why do we have to know the names of a candidate's kids, spouse and family dog? What does the fact that someone is a father and a husband have to do with governing? What does it have to do with virtue? As the Hart case proved — and it was only the most recent example — a campaign photograph doesn't make a family. Journalist Robert Fulford, in an article in *Saturday Night* magazine, said the answer to this conundrum is found in the North American attitude to marriage. Fulford wrote: "North Americans regard marriage as a kind of artifact, or possession, to be judged and assessed by the participants and those who know them." A man is measured by how successful his marriage is, how brilliant his children, how gracious his wife. It is as if his family is a herd of cattle to be assessed and priced on the open market, as if their value reflects his worth.

It is also true that we are naturally curious about the private lives of others, and the success of *People* magazine is testimony to that. But that isn't an excuse, merely an observation. We are curious about a lot of things that are none of our business — our co-workers' sex lives, a neighbour's private grief, someone's struggle with addiction — but that doesn't give us an automatic right to know. We don't quiz our doctor, our insurance adjuster, our garage mechanic about his or her personal life. We would look askance if a doctor's wife or a mechanic's wife started showing up at our appointments, peering over her husband's shoulder and offering sympathy or advice. Why do we tolerate, even expect, this behavior from politicians?

There are those who argue, with some justification, that the way men like Gary Hart or Ted Kennedy treat their wives, in other words the way they function as fathers and husbands, does have political relevance. Certainly, the stories about Hart raised pertinent questions. A lot of liberals shrank from condemning his sexual pyrotechnics for fear of being labelled prudes, so they focused on what became known as "the judgment question" — how could Hart take such foolish risks? But feminists didn't shrink from moral judgment. "There is a kind of implied denigration of women, a lack of respect for the values of women [in Hart's behavior]," said Betty Friedan. What kind of man would humiliate his wife so publicly? How mature is a fifty-year-old man who pursues a series of fleeting relationships with women young enough to be his daughter? Does such a man deserve to be president, where he can do damage to a whole nation of women? These are all valid questions with political ramifications. The press clearly had a right to ask them. Any politician who exploits his wife and family for political advantage deserves to be exposed if his claims aren't true, just as any politician who refuses to drag his family into the limelight deserves to be left alone.

Instructive as the Hart case was, there is a more telling and, ultimately, more important measure of a politician's attitude towards women than his private life, and that is the way he governs. We didn't need Margaret to tell us that Pierre Trudeau is a misogynist; that was evident in the way he ran his government and dealt with women professionally and publicly. Nor can we assume that a politician who is married to a feminist is necessarily going to introduce feminist legislation. Joe Clark didn't, although he wasn't in office very long. It works the other way, too. Brian Mulroney's government has made more progress on women's issues — employment equity legislation, some enlightened judicial appointments, the promise of a national child care system — than its immediate predecessor. Mulroney's advances are still deplorably inadequate, but more than anyone expected of a Tory government. Yet Mulroney, as we have seen, has the most traditional marriage and, one would assume, the most traditional view of women imaginable. When he was still a single, thirty-year-old lawyer practising in Montreal, his mother came to his apartment once a week to pick up his dirty shirts. Then he married Mila, who picked up where his mother left off. Feminism ranks somewhere below solar energy on

Brian's personal agenda. The slight concessions he has made spring not from inner conviction, but from political pressure.

So much for the argument that we need to know everything about the family lives of public figures so that we can smoke out the cheats, the chauvinists and the liars. However interesting such information may be, it does not necessarily help predict political behavior. We should judge politicians on their programs, their promises and their deeds, not on their family lives.

The political system will continue to exploit wives (and families) until women like Lee Hart stop covering up, and until political wives refuse to be paraded around like tame bunnies. Imagine some political wife of the future looking coldly at a reporter, a political organizer, her husband, and stating bluntly, "I'm sorry. I don't wife." It takes courage to resist the pressure to be wifely, especially in official Ottawa, the country's most remote and primitive village. A wife who shuns the political sideshow is often accused of putting her marriage at risk. It happens. More than one cabinet minister with a stay-at-home wife has had an affair with a secretary or an executive assistant — which isn't surprising, since he probably spends more time with his staff than he does with his family. In politics, workaholism is a norm rather than a problem. The job is so demanding it squeezes family life to the margins. If a political wife doesn't follow her husband to the dreary country fairs, tedious dinners and constituency parties, she risks never seeing him.

But is that the wife's problem? Should she be asked to give up her own freedom, her own life to fit into what is an unhealthy pattern? Isn't it about time we retooled political life to accommodate modern families — and not just nuclear families — rather than vice versa?